The XXL Slow Cooker Cookbook

2000 Days of Flavorful and Nutrient-Rich Slow Cooker Recipes to Delight Your Taste Buds

Sarah J. Joyner

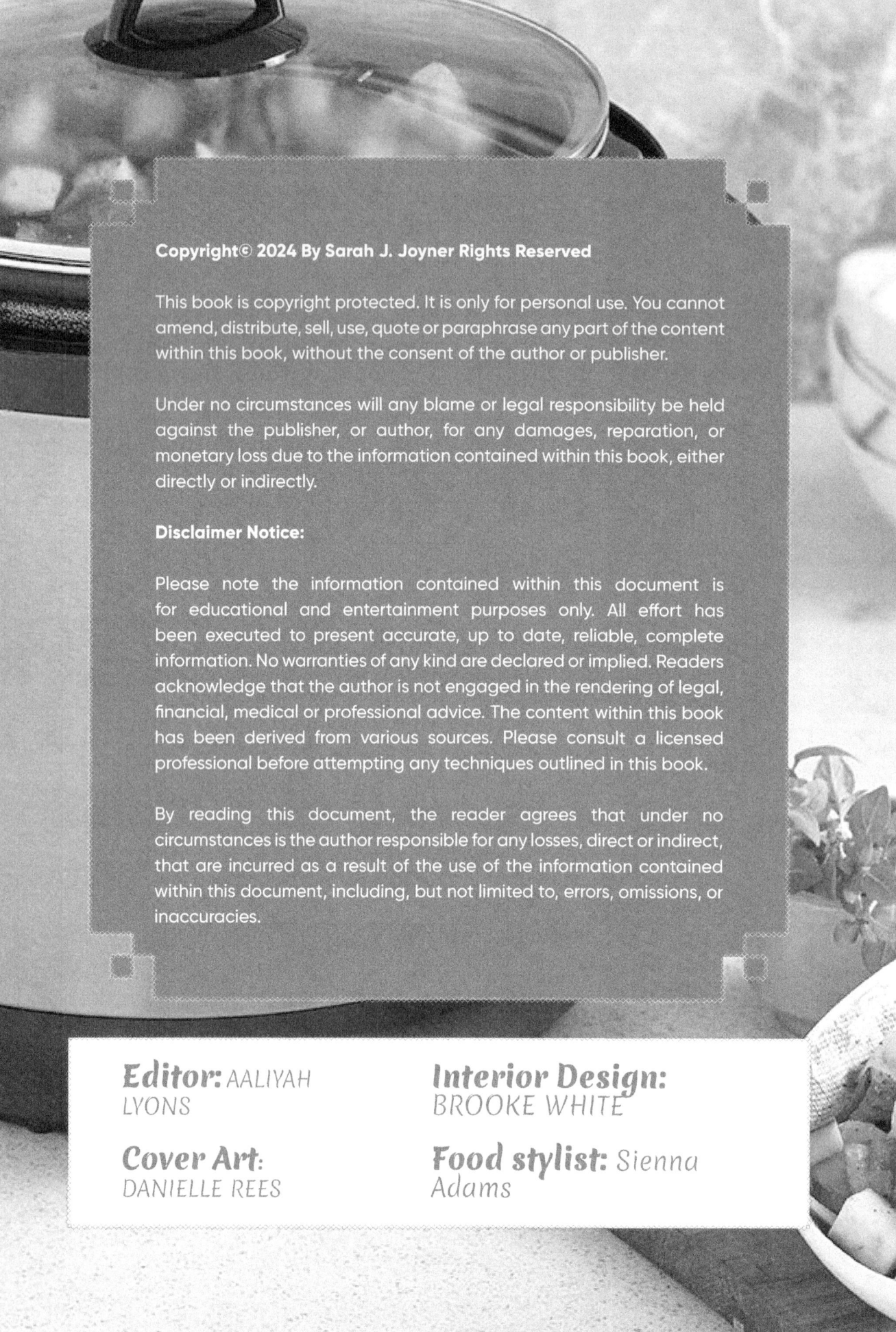

Copyright© 2024 By Sarah J. Joyner Rights Reserved

This book is copyright protected. It is only for personal use. You cannot amend, distribute, sell, use, quote or paraphrase any part of the content within this book, without the consent of the author or publisher.

Under no circumstances will any blame or legal responsibility be held against the publisher, or author, for any damages, reparation, or monetary loss due to the information contained within this book, either directly or indirectly.

Disclaimer Notice:

Please note the information contained within this document is for educational and entertainment purposes only. All effort has been executed to present accurate, up to date, reliable, complete information. No warranties of any kind are declared or implied. Readers acknowledge that the author is not engaged in the rendering of legal, financial, medical or professional advice. The content within this book has been derived from various sources. Please consult a licensed professional before attempting any techniques outlined in this book.

By reading this document, the reader agrees that under no circumstances is the author responsible for any losses, direct or indirect, that are incurred as a result of the use of the information contained within this document, including, but not limited to, errors, omissions, or inaccuracies.

Editor: AALIYAH LYONS

Cover Art: DANIELLE REES

Interior Design: BROOKE WHITE

Food stylist: Sienna Adams

Table Of Contents

Introduction	1
Chapter 1	
The Ultimate Slow Cooker Guide	2
Brief History and Evolution Of Slow Cookers	3
Types of Slow Cookers	4
Essential Tips for Using a Slow Cooker	5
Chapter 2	
Appetizers and Snacks	7
Hot Crab Dip	8
Chili-Cheese Taco Dip	8
Chocolate Peanut Drops	8
Pear & Maple Oatmeal	8
Easy Four-Layer Chocolate Dessert	9
Slow-Cooked Sausage Dressing	9
Almond Banana Bread	10
Sausage Spinach Bake	10
Day After Thanksgiving Cookies	10
Birthday Cake Waffles	11
Seafood Cheese Dip	11
Hot Dried-Beef Dip	11
Coconut Berries Quinoa Mix	12
Almond & Strawberry Oatmeal	12
Creamed Corn	12
Nutella Hand Pies	12
Cheddar Sausage Potatoes	13
Reuben Spread	13
Nacho Hash Brown Casserole	14
Sage Potato Casserole	14
Italian Mushrooms	14
Chapter 3	
Breakfasts and Brunches	15
Pineapple "Baked" Oatmeal	16
Barbecue Sausage Bites	16

Breakfast Casserole	16
Millet Porridge with Dates	17
Date and Nut Loaf	17
Very Vanilla French Toast	17
Sour Cherry & Pumpkin Seed Granola	18
Creamy Cornmeal Porridge	18
Keto Sausage & Egg	18
Corn Cakes with Poached Eggs	19
Slow Cooker Oatmeal	19
Chicago-Style Beef Sandwiches	20
Cheery Cherry Bread	20
Cracked Wheat Porridge	21
Bacon-Mushroom Breakfast	21
Chicken-Apple Breakfast Sausage	21
Hash Brown Pancakes with Smoked Salmon & Dill Cream	22
Overnight Steel-Cut Oats	22
Morning Millet	22
Sweet Breakfast Grits	22
Egg & Mushroom Breakfast	23
Breakfast Oatmeal	23
Banana Loaf	23
Caramel-Apple Oats	24
Vegetarian Stew in Bread Bowls	24
Golden Beet & Spinach Frittata	24

Chapter 4
Poultry — 25

Pork and Green Chili Stew	26
Chicken Tortilla Casserole	26
Savory Slow Cooker Chicken	27
Mandarin Turkey Tenderloin	27
Lemony Herbs Chicken	27
Salsa Turkey Loaf	28
Queso Chicken Tacos	28
Asian Meatballs	29
Garlic Herb Roasted Pepper Chicken	29
Slow Cook Turkey Breast	30
Chili-Lime Chicken Tostadas	30
Tandoori Chicken Panini	30
Creamy Chicken Curry	31
Parmesan Chicken Rice	31
Chicken and Bean Torta	31
Red-Cooked Chicken	32
Chicken Curry	33
Bavarian Pot Roast	33
Simple Chicken & Mushrooms	34
Easy Mexican Chicken	34
Southwest Chicken	34
Chicken-Vegetable Dish	35
Mango & Grilled Chicken Salad	35
Chinese Poached Chicken	35
Rosemary Lemon Wings	36
Cape Breton Chicken	36
Chicken Soft Tacos	36

Chapter 5
Beef, Pork and Lamb — 37

Chicago-Style Italian Beef	38
Java Roast Beef	38
Beer-Braised Stew	39
Beef and Artichokes Bowls	39
Sweet and Spicy Jerk Ribs	39
Easy Meatball Stroganoff	40
Salsa Beef Fajitas	40
Fruited Flank Steak	40
Beef and Scallions Bowl	41
Balsamic Beef	41
Barbacoa Lamb	41
Pork Tenderloin Braised In Milk with Fresh Herbs	42
Pacific Rim Braised Short Ribs	42
Cheeseburger Skillet Dinner	43
Mahogany Glazed Pork	43
Mustard Beef	43
Lamb with Mint and Green Beans	44
Slow-Cooked Pork and Beans	44
Cilantro Beef	44
Tender Texas-Style Steaks	45
Breaded Pork Tenderloin	45
Succulent Lamb	45
Pub-Crawl Short Ribs	46
Pork Chops with Tomato Sauce and Mushrooms	46
Onion Beef	47
Slow Cooker Sauerbraten	47

Chapter 6
Fish and Seafood — 48

Chicken and Shrimp Casserole	49
Shrimp Creole	49
Poached Salmon in Court-Bouillon Recipe	49
Soy-Ginger Steamed Pompano	50
Beantown Scallops	50
Garlic Shrimp	50
Salmon Poached in White Wine	51
Shrimp Marinara	51
Southwestern Fish Tacos	51
Clam Chowder	52
Chicken and Shrimp Jambalaya	52
Company Seafood Pasta	52
Soy Steamed Pompano	53
Vietnamese Braised Catfish	53
Vietnamese Catfish	53
Chili Shrimps	54
Spicy Shrimps	54
Garlic Crab Claws	54
Braised Squid with Tomatoes and Fennel	54
Lemon Pepper Tilapia	55
Crab Cioppino	55
Garlic Salmon Linguine	56
Shrimp Creole Stew	56
Shrimp Jambalaya	57
Confetti Seafood Chowder	57

Chapter 7
Rice, Grains, and Beans — 58

Kale & White Bean Chili	59
Super Green Beans	59
Balsamic-Glazed Beets	59
Cheesy Slow Cooker Pizza	60
Pasta Sauce with Meat and Veggies	60
Green Chile and Sour Cream Rice Casserole	60
Greek-Style Green Beans	61
Slow-Cooked Wild Rice	61
Herbed Harvest Rice	61
Special Green Beans	62
Barbecued Baked Beans	62
Coconutty Brown Rice	62
Cauliflower Rice and Spinach	62
Chicken and Triple Mushroom Casserole	63
Easy Baked Beans	63
Slimmed-Down Spaghetti Sauce	63
Barbecued Green Beans	64
Herby Slow Cooker Pizza	64
Fiesta Corn and Beans	64

Chapter 8
Vegan and Vegetarian — 65

Zuppa Toscana	66
Green Pea Casserole	66
Cheesy Beer Dip Salsa	66
Creamy Mashed Potatoes	66
Creamy Carrot Casserole	67
Elbows Casserole	67
Asian-Style Broccoli	67
Golden Cauliflower	67
Indian-Spiced Cauliflower	68
Apricot-Glazed Carrots	68
Braised Cabbage	68
Maple-Dijon Brussels Sprouts	69
Golden Carrots	69
Brussels Sprout Dip	69
Garlic Mashed Potatoes	69
Balsamic Beets	70
Broccoli Delight	70
Lentil Bolognese	70

Chapter 9
Soups, Stews and Chilis — 71

Anything Goes Sausage Soup	72
Wintertime Meatball Soup	72
Ginger Pear Pumpkin Soup	72
Roasted Tomato Soup with Spinach Pesto	73
Delicious Chicken Soup with Lemongrass	73
Bone Broth	74
Creamy Loaded Baked-Potato Soup	74
Lotsa-Tomatoes Beef Stew	75
Italian Chicken Stew	75
Beef Barley Vegetable Soup	75

Pumpkin Turkey Chili	76
Chipotle Chicken Chili	76
White Chicken Chili	77
Fennel Flavored Fish Stew	77
Julia's Potato and Leek Soup	78
White Chili	78
Simple Texas Chili	78
Creamy Broccoli Soup	79
Slow Cooker Pork Stew with Tapioca	79
Golden Lentil Soup	79

Chapter 10
Desserts 80
Slow Cooker Apple Pudding Cake	81
Fresh Apricot Jam	81
Rhubarb-Strawberry Compote	82
Easy Chocolate Cheesecake	82
Chocolate Chip Brownie	83
Spiced Sweet Potato Pudding	83
Caramel Pear Pudding	83
Slow Cooker Baked Apples	84
Fruity Delight Cake	84
Stewed Blueberries	84
Fresh Bing Cherry Jam	85
Choco Lava Cake	85
Stuffed Sweet Onions	85
Rum-Butterscotch Bananas	86
Slow-Cooked Bread Pudding	86
Lemon Poppy Seed Upside-Down Cake	86
Coconut Cupcakes	87
Fig and Ginger Jam	87

Appendix 1 Measurement Conversion Chart	88
Appendix 2 The Dirty Dozen and Clean Fifteen	89
Appendix 3 Index	90

Introduction

Welcome to "The XXL Slow Cooker Cookbook," where the art of slow cooking meets the joy of preparing delicious, comforting meals with ease. In this culinary journey, we invite you to explore the world of tantalizing flavors, mouthwatering aromas, and the unrivaled convenience of slow-cooked cuisine.

Slow cooking has long been celebrated for its unique ability to transform humble ingredients into extraordinary dishes. Whether you're a seasoned home cook or someone just beginning to explore the wonders of the kitchen, the slow cooker is a versatile tool that will quickly become your trusted kitchen companion. It's a device that makes time your ally, allowing you to effortlessly create culinary masterpieces.

In today's fast-paced world, where the demands of daily life often leave us with little time to prepare wholesome, homemade meals, the slow cooker shines as a beacon of hope. "The XXL Slow Cooker Cookbook" has been meticulously crafted to help you unlock the full potential of this wonderful appliance, making your busy life a little easier and a lot more delicious.

One of the great joys of slow cooking is the tantalizing anticipation that builds as your meal slowly simmers and fills your home with enchanting scents. Whether it's the hearty aroma of a comforting stew, the exotic spices of a savory curry, or the sweet scent of a dessert in the making, your senses will be captivated by the transformation taking place inside your slow cooker.

This cookbook is a celebration of the diverse world of slow-cooked cuisine. within its pages, you'll find an array of recipes that cater to different tastes and dietary preferences. From traditional comfort foods that evoke memories of family gatherings to modern, globally inspired dishes that will expand your culinary horizons, there's something for everyone.

The beauty of slow cooking lies not only in its ability to create delicious meals but also in its practicality. with a few simple preparations, you can set your ingredients in the slow cooker and go about your day, knowing that dinner is well underway. It's an ideal solution for busy individuals and families looking for a convenient way to enjoy homemade, wholesome food.

In "The XXL Slow Cooker Cookbook," you'll find a treasure trove of recipes that showcase the potential of slow cooking for every occasion. Whether you're hosting a dinner party, planning a romantic meal for two, or simply looking for no-fuss weeknight dinners, you'll discover a wealth of ideas that will make your culinary aspirations a reality.

As you embark on this slow-cooking adventure, you'll also learn valuable tips and tricks to make the most of your slow cooker. From selecting the right cuts of meat to achieving the perfect balance of seasonings, these insights will help you master the art of slow cooking and impress your family and friends with your culinary prowess.

We hope that "The XXL Slow Cooker Cookbook" becomes an indispensable part of your kitchen, inspiring you to create memorable dishes that bring people together. Slow cooking isn't just about food; it's about the joy of sharing, the comfort of home, and the warmth of a homemade meal.

So, whether you're a busy professional, a parent juggling multiple responsibilities, or simply someone who appreciates the ease and elegance of slow-cooked dishes, this cookbook is your ticket to a world of culinary delight. Embrace the simplicity, savor the flavors, and relish the convenience of slow cooking. Bon appétit!

Chapter 1

The Ultimate Slow Cooker Guide

Brief History and Evolution Of Slow Cookers

A GLIMPSE INTO THE PAST: THE EVOLUTION OF SLOW COOKERS

In today's fast-paced world, slow cookers have become a ubiquitous appliance in kitchens around the globe. These unassuming devices simplify the art of cooking, transforming humble ingredients into mouthwatering meals with minimal effort. But the history of slow cookers is a tale of innovation, convenience, and the quest for flavorful, fuss-free cuisine.

The concept of slow cooking has ancient roots. Before the invention of modern appliances, people practiced slow cooking over open flames, in hearths, or using rudimentary clay pots. It was a method driven by necessity and a deep understanding of how long, slow simmering could transform tough cuts of meat and simple ingredients into culinary delights.

However, the transition from traditional cooking methods to the modern slow cooker we know today was a gradual process.

EARLY PRECURSORS TO THE SLOW COOKER

The precursor to the slow cooker can be traced back to 1950s America. During this time, a man named Irving Naxon patented a device called the "Naxon Beanery," which was inspired by a traditional Jewish Sabbath stew called cholent. This early slow cooker was a ceramic pot encased in a metal casing. It was designed to be left unattended for long periods, just like the Sabbath stew, and relied on low heat to cook food slowly.

Despite his invention, Naxon struggled to gain attention for his device. It wasn't until the 1970s that interest in slow cooking began to grow.

THE RISE OF THE CROCK-POT

The 1970s saw the emergence of the iconic Crock-Pot, a brand that would become synonymous with slow cooking. The Crock-Pot was invented by Robert C. W. Irvine, and his creation was marketed as a convenient solution for busy households. It featured a removable stoneware insert that could be used as a cooking vessel and for serving, making cleanup a breeze.

The Crock-Pot's success can be attributed to the changing dynamics of American households. As more women entered the workforce, the need for convenient, time-saving cooking methods became evident. The Crock-Pot's "set it and forget it" approach struck a chord with families seeking a way to prepare hearty, home-cooked meals without being tethered to the stove.

By the 1980s, the Crock-Pot had become an integral part of American kitchens, with an array of recipe books and cookware accessories to support its use.

MODERN SLOW COOKERS AND ADVANCEMENTS

Today, slow cookers have evolved to include a wide range of features and sizes. Traditional slow cookers are still available, with manual controls and basic settings. However, the market has expanded to include programmable models that offer greater control over cooking times and temperatures. Multi-cookers, such as the popular Instant Pot, often include a slow cooker function, further diversifying the options available to consumers.

The materials used in slow cookers have also changed. While early models often featured stoneware inserts, many modern slow cookers utilize stainless steel or non-stick coatings, making them easier to clean and more durable.

Types of Slow Cookers

EXPLORING THE WORLD OF SLOW COOKERS: TYPES AND FEATURES

Slow cookers, also known as Crock-Pots in some regions, have come a long way since their humble beginnings. Today, there are several types of slow cookers available on the market, each offering distinct features to cater to the diverse needs of home cooks. Let's delve into the world of slow cookers and explore their different types.

1. Traditional Slow Cookers:
Traditional slow cookers are the pioneers of the genre. They typically consist of a ceramic or stoneware insert that sits in a metal or plastic housing. These slow cookers come in various sizes, including 2-quart, 4-quart, 6-quart, and larger options, making them versatile for preparing meals of different portions. They have manual controls, usually featuring three temperature settings: low, high, and warm. These simple yet effective appliances are perfect for those who appreciate the classic, hands-on approach to slow cooking.

2. Programmable Slow Cookers:
Programmable slow cookers offer a more advanced level of control compared to their traditional counterparts. They include digital displays and timers, allowing you to set specific cooking times and temperatures. Once the cooking time is up, these slow cookers automatically switch to the warm setting, ensuring your meal stays hot and ready to serve. Programmable slow cookers are ideal for busy individuals who want to enjoy the convenience of coming home to a hot, well-cooked meal.

3. Multi-Cookers with Slow Cooking Function:
Multi-cookers have gained popularity in recent years for their versatility. These kitchen appliances combine various functions, such as slow cooking, pressure cooking, sautéing, and more. The Instant Pot, a well-known multi-cooker, is a prime example. Multi-cookers often come with preset cooking programs, making it easy to switch between functions. While they excel at slow cooking, their ability to perform a wide range of cooking techniques makes them an attractive option for home cooks who want an all-in-one solution.

4. Connectable Slow Cookers:
Connectable slow cookers offer the flexibility to cook multiple dishes simultaneously. These slow cookers consist of two or more separate cooking units that can be connected to a single base. Each unit operates independently, allowing you to prepare different dishes at the same time. Connectable slow cookers are

excellent for potlucks, gatherings, or when you have varying dietary preferences to accommodate.

5. Casserole Slow Cookers:
Casserole slow cookers are designed to resemble a traditional casserole dish. They are typically compact and have a sleek design that allows them to double as a serving dish. These slow cookers are perfect for preparing smaller portions of food or dishes that require minimal cooking time. The convenience of cooking and serving in the same container makes them a favorite among those who appreciate simplicity.

6. Travel Slow Cookers:
Travel slow cookers are tailor-made for those who are constantly on the move. They come with secure lids and are designed to be portable, making them ideal for taking your slow-cooked meals to potlucks, picnics, or road trips. Many travel slow cookers also feature clamps or seals to prevent spills during transportation.

7. Advanced Smart Slow Cookers:
In the age of smart technology, slow cookers have joined the revolution. Smart slow cookers can be controlled and monitored remotely through smartphone apps. They allow you to adjust cooking settings and check the progress of your meal from anywhere, providing the ultimate level of convenience and flexibility.

Essential Tips for Using a Slow Cooker

MASTERING THE ART OF SLOW COOKING: ESSENTIAL TIPS FOR SUCCESS
Slow cookers, with their set-it-and-forget-it approach, have become a kitchen essential for busy individuals and families seeking convenient, homemade meals. To make the most of your slow cooker and create dishes bursting with flavor and tenderness, it's essential to understand some key tips and techniques. Here are the essential tips for using a slow cooker successfully.

CHOOSE THE RIGHT SIZE
Slow cookers come in various sizes, from small 2-quart models to larger 8-quart ones. Select a size that suits your family's needs and the types of meals you want to prepare. Overfilling or under-filling the slow cooker can affect the cooking process and the final results.

PREPARING INGREDIENTS
While slow cookers are known for their convenience, they still require some prep work. Trim excess fat from meat, chop vegetables, and season ingredients as necessary. Browning meat in a skillet before adding it to the slow cooker can enhance flavor and texture.

LAYER INGREDIENTS WISELY
To ensure even cooking and proper distribution of flavors, layer your ingredients correctly. Place denser, slow-cooking vegetables at the bottom and meat on top. This helps prevent overcooking or undercooking.

USE THE RIGHT LIQUID

Slow cookers retain moisture exceptionally well, so you often need less liquid than in traditional cooking methods. Aim for about half the amount of liquid you would use for stovetop or oven cooking. Avoid overcrowding with liquid, as it can lead to a watery result.

DON'T PEEK TOO OFTEN

Resisting the temptation to lift the lid is crucial. Each time you do, heat escapes, extending the cooking time. Only open the lid when necessary, such as to add last-minute ingredients or check for doneness.

ADJUST SEASONING

Herbs and spices can lose their potency during long, slow cooking. It's a good idea to add seasonings toward the end of the cooking time for a fresher taste. Taste and adjust the seasonings before serving.

CHOOSE THE RIGHT CUT OF MEAT

Tough cuts of meat, like chuck roast or pork shoulder, are ideal for slow cooking. The long cooking time allows the collagen to break down, resulting in tender, flavorful dishes.

BE MINDFUL OF DAIRY AND SEAFOOD

Dairy products, such as milk or cream, and seafood, like shrimp or fish, cook much faster than other ingredients in a slow cooker. Add them during the final hour to prevent overcooking and curdling.

AVOID EXCESSIVE FATS

While a certain amount of fat is necessary for flavor, too much can lead to greasy dishes. Trim excess fat from meat before cooking or skim the fat off the surface during cooking.

CLEANING AND MAINTENANCE

After your meal, unplug the slow cooker and let it cool before cleaning. Most slow cooker inserts are dishwasher safe, making cleanup a breeze. For stubborn residue, soaking with warm, soapy water can help.

KNOW YOUR SLOW COOKER'S TEMPERATURES

Slow cookers vary in their temperature settings. Some may cook at a higher or lower temperature than expected. Get to know your specific model to adjust cooking times accordingly.

PLAN FOR COOKING TIME

Slow cooking is not suitable for last-minute meals. Plan your slow cooker dishes well in advance, as most recipes require several hours of cooking time. It's a great way to prepare for busy days or have a meal ready when you return home.

SAFE HANDLING

Food safety is paramount. Always store perishable ingredients in the refrigerator until you're ready to cook. Avoid placing frozen ingredients directly into the slow cooker to prevent bacteria growth. Thaw them in the refrigerator first.

EXPERIMENT AND ADAPT

Slow cooking is an art, and there's room for creativity. Don't be afraid to experiment with ingredients and flavors. Adapt recipes to your preferences and dietary needs.

Chapter 2

Appetizers and Snacks

Hot Crab Dip

Prep time: 5 minutes | Cook time: 3 hours | Makes 5 cups

- 1/2 cup milk
- 1/3 cup salsa
- 3 packages (8 ounces each) cream cheese, cubed
- 2 packages (8 ounces each) imitation crabmeat, flaked
- 1 cup thinly sliced green onions
- 1 can (4 ounces) chopped green chilies
- assorted crackers

1. In a small bowl, combine milk and salsa. Transfer to a greased 3-qt. slow cooker. Stir in cream cheese, crab, onions and chilies.
2. Cover and cook on low for 3-4 hours, stirring every 30 minutes. Serve with crackers.

Chili-Cheese Taco Dip

Prep time: 15 minutes | Cook time: 1-1½ hours | Serves 10-12

- 1 lb. ground beef
- 1 can chili, without beans
- 1 lb. mild Mexican cheese
- Velveeta cheese, cubed

1. Brown beef, crumble into small pieces, and drain.
2. Combine beef, chili, and cheese in slow cooker.
3. Cover. Cook on Low 1-1½ hours, or until cheese is melted, stirring occasionally to blend ingredients.
4. Serve warm with taco or tortilla chips.

Chocolate Peanut Drops

Prep time: 20 minutes | Cook time: 1½ hours | Makes 11 dozen

- 4 ounces German sweet chocolate, chopped
- 1 package (12 ounces) semisweet chocolate chips
- 4 packages (10 to 12 ounces each) white baking chips
- 2 jars (16 ounces each) lightly salted dry roasted peanuts

1. In a 6-qt. slow cooker, layer in order listed (do not stir). Cover and cook on low for 1½ hours. Stir to combine. (If chocolate is not melted, cover and cook 15 minutes longer; stir. Repeat in 15-minute increments until chocolate is melted.)
2. Drop mixture by rounded tablespoonfuls onto waxed paper. Let stand until set. Store in an airtight container at room temperature.

Pear & Maple Oatmeal

Prep time: 10 minutes | Cook time: 7 hours | Serves 2

- 1½ cups milk
- ½ cup steel cut oats
- ½ tsp vanilla extract
- 1 pear, chopped
- ½ tsp maple extract
- 1 tbsp sugar

1. In your slow cooker, combine milk with oats, vanilla, pear, maple extract and sugar, stir, cover and cook on Low for 7 hours.
2. Divide into bowls and serve for breakfast.

8 | The XXL Slow Cooker Cookbook

Easy Four-Layer Chocolate Dessert

Prep time: 25 minutes | Cook time: 15 minutes | Serves 15

- 1 cup all-purpose flour
- $1/2$ cup cold butter
- 1 cup chopped walnuts, toasted, divided
- 1 pkg. (8 oz.) cream cheese, softened
- 1 cup confectioners' sugar
- 2 cartons (8 oz. each) frozen whipped topping, thawed, divided
- $2 1/2$ cups 2% milk
- 2 pkg. (3.9 oz. each) instant chocolate pudding mix
- 1 cup semisweet chocolate chunks
- chocolate syrup

1. Preheat oven to 350°. Place flour in a small bowl; cut in butter until crumbly. Stir in $1/2$ cup walnuts. Press onto bottom of an ungreased 13x9-in. baking dish. Bake until light golden brown, 12-15 minutes. Cool completely on a wire rack.
2. In a small bowl, beat cream cheese and confectioners' sugar until smooth; fold in one carton whipped topping.
3. Spread over crust. In a large bowl, whisk milk and pudding mix 2 minutes. Gently spread over cream cheese layer. Top with remaining whipped topping. Sprinkle with chocolate chunks and remaining walnuts. Refrigerate until cold.
4. Cut into bars. Just before serving, drizzle with chocolate syrup.

Slow-Cooked Sausage Dressing

Prep time: 20 minutes | Cook time: 3 hours | Makes 8 cups

- 1/2 pound reduced-fat bulk pork sausage
- 2 celery ribs, chopped
- 1 large onion, chopped
- 7 cups seasoned stuffing cubes
- 1 can (14 $1/2$ ounces) reduced-sodium chicken broth
- 1 medium tart apple, chopped
- $1/3$ cup chopped pecans
- 2 tablespoons reduced-fat butter, melted
- $1 1/2$ teaspoons rubbed sage
- $1/2$ teaspoon pepper

1. In a large nonstick skillet, cook the sausage, celery and onion over medium heat until meat is no longer pink; drain. Transfer to a large bowl; stir in the remaining.
2. Place in a 5-qt. slow cooker coated with cooking spray. Cover and cook on low for 3-4 hours or until heated through and the apple is tender, stirring once.

Almond Banana Bread

Prep time: 10 minutes | Cook time: 4 hours | Serves 2

- 1 egg
- 2 tbsp butter, melted
- ½ cup sugar
- 1 cup flour
- ½ tsp baking powder
- ¼ tsp baking soda
- a pinch of cinnamon powder
- a pinch of nutmeg, ground
- 2 bananas, mashed
- ¼ cup almonds, sliced
- cooking spray

1. In a bowl, mix sugar with flour, baking powder, baking soda, cinnamon and nutmeg and stir.
2. Add egg, butter, almonds and bananas and stir really well.
3. Grease your slow cooker with cooking spray, pour bread mix, cover and cook on Low for 4 hours.
4. Slice bread and serve for breakfast.

Sausage Spinach Bake

Prep time: 20 minutes | Cook time: 40 minutes | Serves 12

- 1 pkg. (6 oz.) savory herb-flavored stuffing mix
- ½ lb. bulk pork sausage
- ¼ cup chopped green onions
- ½ tsp. minced garlic
- 1 pkg. (10 oz.) frozen chopped spinach, thawed and squeezed dry
- 1½ cups shredded monterey jack cheese
- 1½ cups half-and-half cream
- 3 large eggs
- 2 tbsp. grated Parmesan cheese

1. Prepare stuffing according to package directions. Meanwhile, crumble sausage into a large skillet. Add onions; cook over medium heat until meat is no longer pink. Add garlic; cook 1 minute longer. Drain.
2. In a large bowl, combine the stuffing, sausage mixture and spinach. Transfer to a greased 11x7-in. baking dish; sprinkle with shredded Monterey Jack cheese. In a small bowl, combine cream and eggs; pour over sausage mixture.
3. Bake at 400° until a thermometer reads 160°, 35-40 minutes. Sprinkle with grated Parmesan cheese; bake until bubbly, about 5 minutes longer.

Day After Thanksgiving Cookies

Prep time: 25 minutes | Cook time: 15 minutes | Makes about 6 dozen

- 1 cup butter, softened
- 1 cup sugar
- 1 cup packed brown sugar
- ¾ cup canned pumpkin pie filling
- 1 tsp. baking soda
- ½ tsp. salt
- ½ tsp. ground nutmeg
- ¼ tsp. ground cloves
- 1 cup white baking chips
- 1 cup semisweet chocolate chips

1. In a large bowl, cream butter and sugars until light and fluffy. Beat in pumpkin pie filling, cranberry sauce, egg and vanilla.
2. Preheat oven to 350°. Drop dough by rounded tablespoonfuls 2 in. apart onto ungreased baking sheets. Bake until edges are golden brown, 15-18 minutes. Cool on pans 5 minutes; remove from pans to wire racks to cool completely.

Birthday Cake Waffles

Prep time: 20 minutes | Cook time: 25 minutes | Makes 6 waffles

- 1 cup all-purpose flour
- 1 cup (about 5 oz.) confetti cake mix or flavor of choice
- 2 tbsp. cornstarch
- 3 tsp. baking powder
- 1/4 tsp. salt
- 2 tbsp. rainbow sprinkles, optional
- 2 large eggs
- 1 3/4 cups 2% milk
- 3/4 to 1 cup plain greek yogurt
- 1/2 tsp. vanilla extract
- 1/2 tsp. almond extract

Cream Cheese Frosting:
- 4 oz. softened cream cheese or reduced-fat cream cheese
- 1/4 cup butter, softened
- 1 1/2 to 2 cups confectioners' sugar
- 1/2 tsp. vanilla extract
- 1 to 3 tbsp. 2% milk

1. Preheat oven to 300°. Combine the first five ingredients and, if desired, rainbow sprinkles. In another bowl, whisk eggs, milk, yogurt and extracts. Add yogurt mixture to flour mixture; mix until smooth.
2. Preheat waffle maker coated with cooking spray. Pour batter and bake waffles according to the manufacturer's directions until golden brown. Transfer cooked waffles to oven until ready to serve.
3. For frosting, beat cream cheese and butter on high until light and fluffy, 2-3 minutes. Gradually beat in confectioners' sugar, 1/2 cup at a time, until smooth. Beat in vanilla. Add enough milk to reach desired consistency. Spread over warm waffles.

For a cakelike look, cut waffles into fourths and stack them; decorate with birthday candles.

Seafood Cheese Dip

Prep time: 15 minutes | Cook time: 1 1/2 hours | Makes 5 cups

- 1 package (32 ounces) process cheese (Velveeta), cubed
- 2 cans (6 ounces each) lump crabmeat, drained
- 1 can (10 ounces) diced tomatoes and green chilies, undrained
- 1 cup frozen cooked salad shrimp, thawed
- french bread baguettes, sliced and toasted

1. In a greased 3-qt. slow cooker, combine the cheese, crab, tomatoes and shrimp.
2. Cover and cook on low for 1 1/2 to 2 hours or until cheese is melted, stirring occasionally. Serve with baguettes.

Hot Dried-Beef Dip

Prep time: 30 minutes | Cook time: 2-3 hours | Serves 12-15

- 2 8-oz. pkgs. cream cheese, softened
- 8 ozs. cheddar cheese, shredded
- 1 green pepper, chopped fine
- 1 small onion, chopped fine
- ¼ lb. dried beef, shredded

1. In a medium-sized mixing bowl, combine cream cheese and shredded cheese.
2. Fold in peppers, onions, and dried beef. Place stiff mixture in slow cooker.
3. Cover and cook on Low 2-3 hours. Stir occasionally.
4. Serve hot with crackers.

Coconut Berries Quinoa Mix

Prep time: 10 minutes | Cook time: 8 hours | Serves 2

- ½ cup quinoa
- 1 cup water
- ½ cup coconut milk
- 1 tbsp maple syrup
- 1 tbsp mix berries

1. In your slow cooker, mix quinoa with water, coconut milk, maple syrup and salt, stir well, cover and cook on Low for 8 hours.
2. Divide into 2 bowls, sprinkle berries on top and serve for breakfast.

Almond & Strawberry Oatmeal

Prep time: 10 minutes | Cook time: 6 hours | Serves 2

- 1 cup steel cut oats
- 3 cups water
- 1 cup almond milk
- 1 cup strawberries, chopped
- ½ cup Greek yogurt
- ½ tsp cinnamon powder
- ½ tsp vanilla extract

1. In your slow cooker, mix oats with water, milk, strawberries, yogurt, cinnamon and vanilla, toss, cover and cook on Low for 6 hours.
2. Stir your oatmeal one more time, divide into bowls and serve for breakfast.

Creamed Corn

Prep time: 10 minutes | Cook time: 3 hours | Serves 5

- 2 packages (one 16 ounces, one 10 ounces) frozen corn
- 1 package (8 ounces) cream cheese, softened and cubed
- ¼ cup butter, cubed
- 1 tablespoon sugar
- ½ teaspoon salt

1. In a 3-qt. slow cooker coated with cooking spray, combine all the.
2. Cover and cook on low for 3 to 3 ½ hours or until cheese is melted and corn is tender.
3. Stir just before serving.

Nutella Hand Pies

Prep time: 30 minutes | Cook time: 30 minutes | Serves 9

- 1 large egg
- 1 tbsp. water
- 1 sheet frozen puff pastry, thawed
- 3 tbsp. nutella
- 1 to 2 tsp. grated orange zest

Icing:
- ⅓ cup confectioners' sugar
- ½ tsp. orange juice
- ⅛ tsp. grated orange zest
- additional nutella, optional

1. Preheat oven to 400°. In a small bowl, whisk egg with water.
2. Unfold puff pastry; cut into nine squares. Place 1 tsp. Nutella in center of each; sprinkle with orange zest. Brush edges of pastry with egg mixture.
3. Fold one corner over filling to form a triangle; press edges to seal. Transfer to an ungreased baking sheet.
4. Bake until golden brown and pastry has cooked through, 17-20 minutes. Cool slightly.
5. In a small bowl, mix confectioners' sugar, orange juice and orange zest; drizzle over pies. If desired, warm additional Nutella in a microwave and drizzle over tops.

Cheddar Sausage Potatoes

Prep time: 10 minutes | Cook time: 4 hours | Serves 2

- 2 potatoes, chopped
- ½ red bell pepper, chopped
- ½ green bell pepper, chopped
- ½ yellow onion, chopped
- 4 oz smoked Italian sausage, sliced
- 1 cup cheddar cheese, shredded
- ¼ cup sour cream
- A pinch of oregano, dried
- ¼ tsp basil, dried
- 4 oz chicken cream
- 1 tbsp parsley, chopped

1. Put the potato in your slow cooker, add red bell pepper, green bell pepper, onion, sausage, cheese, sour cream, oregano, basil, and chicken cream, cover and cook on Low for 4 hours.
2. Add parsley, toss, divide between plates and serve for breakfast.

Hamburger-Cheese Dip

Prep time: 20 minutes | Cook time: 2-3 hours | Serves 8-10

- 1 lb. ground beef, browned and crumbled into small pieces
- ½ tsp. salt
- ½ cup chopped green peppers
- ¾ cup chopped onion
- 8-oz. can tomato sauce
- 4-oz. can green chilies, chopped
- 1 tbsp. Worcestershire sauce
- 1 tbsp. brown sugar
- 1 lb. Velveeta cheese, cubed
- 1 tbsp. paprika
- red pepper to taste

1. Combine beef, salt, green peppers, onion, tomato sauce, green chilies, Worcestershire sauce, and brown sugar in slow cooker.
2. Cover. Cook on Low 2-3 hours. During the last hour stir in cheese, paprika, and red pepper.
3. Serve with tortilla chips.

Reuben Spread

Prep time: 10 minutes | Cook time: 4 hours | Serves 30

- 2 packages (8 ounces each) cream cheese, cubed
- 4 cups (16 ounces) shredded Swiss cheese
- 1 can (14 ounces) sauerkraut, rinsed and well drained
- 4 packages (2 ounces each) thinly sliced deli corned beef, chopped
- ½ cup Thousand Island salad dressing
- snack rye bread or rye crackers

1. Place the first five in a 1½-qt. slow cooker; stir to combine. Cook, covered, on low 4 to 4½ hours or until heated through.
2. Stir to blend. Serve spread with bread.

Nacho Hash Brown Casserole

Prep time: 15 minutes | Cook time: 3 1/4 hours | Serves 8

- 1 package (32 ounces) frozen cubed hash brown potatoes, thawed
- 1 can (10 3/4 ounces) condensed cream of celery soup, undiluted
- 1 can (10 3/4 ounces) condensed nacho cheese soup, undiluted
- 1 large onion, finely chopped
- 1/3 cup butter, melted
- 1 cup (8 ounces) reduced-fat sour cream

1. In a greased 3-qt. slow cooker, combine the first five.
2. Cover and cook on low for 3-4 hours or until potatoes are tender.
3. Stir in sour cream. Cover and cook 15-30 minutes longer or until heated through.

Sage Potato Casserole

Prep time: 10 minutes | Cook time: 3 hours and 30 minutes | Serves 2

- 1 tsp onion powder
- 3 eggs, whisked
- ½ tsp garlic powder
- ½ tsp sage, dried
- 2 garlic cloves, minced
- a pinch of red pepper flakes
- ½ tbsp olive oil
- 2 red potatoes, cubed

1. Grease your slow cooker with the oil, add potatoes, onion, garlic, parsley and pepper flakes and toss a bit.
2. In a bowl, mix eggs with onion powder, garlic powder, sage, salt and pepper, whisk well and pour over potatoes.
3. Cover, cook on High for 3 hours and 30 minutes, divide into 2 plates and serve for breakfast.

Super-Bowl Dip

Prep time: 15 minutes | Cook time: 2-3 hours | Serves 30

- 2 lbs. ground beef
- 1 envelope dry taco seasoning mix
- 24-oz. jar salsa, your choice of heat
- 1 lb. Velveeta cheese, cubed
- oz. can refried beans

1. Brown beef in nonstick skillet. Drain.
2. Place beef in slow cooker. Stir in remaining ingredients.
3. Cover and cook on Low 2-3 hours, or until cheese is melted.
4. Serve with tortilla chips.

Italian Mushrooms

Prep time: 10 minutes | Cook time: 4 hours | Serves 6

- 1 pound medium fresh mushrooms
- 1 large onion, sliced
- ½ cup butter, melted
- 1 envelope Italian salad dressing mix

1. In a 3-qt. slow cooker, layer mushrooms and onion.
2. Combine butter and salad dressing mix; pour over vegetables.
3. Cover and cook on low for 4-5 hours or until vegetables are tender. Serve with a slotted spoon.

Chapter 3

Breakfasts and Brunches

Pineapple "Baked" Oatmeal

Prep time: 5 minutes | Cook time: 1½-2½ hours | Serves 5-6

- 1 box of 8 instant oatmeal packets (approx. a 12- to 14-oz. box), any flavor
- 1½ tsp. baking powder
- 2 eggs, beaten
- ½ cup milk
- 8-oz. can crushed pineapple in juice, undrained

1. Spray inside of slow cooker with nonstick cooking spray.
2. Empty packets of oatmeal into a large bowl. Add baking powder and mix.
3. Stir in eggs, milk, and undrained pineapple.
4. Mix well. Pour mixture into slow cooker. Cover and cook on High 1½ hours, or on Low 2½ hours.

Barbecue Sausage Bites

Prep time: 10 minutes | Cook time: 2½ hours | Serves 12-14

- 1 package (16 ounces) miniature smoked sausages
- ¾ pound fully cooked bratwurst links, cut into ½-inch slices
- ¾ pound smoked kielbasa or Polish sausage, cut into ½-inch slices
- 1 bottle (18 ounces) barbecue sauce
- ⅔ cup orange marmalade
- ½ teaspoon ground mustard
- ⅛ teaspoon ground allspice
- 1 can (20 ounces) pineapple chunks, drained

1. In a 3-qt. slow cooker, combine the sausages. In a small bowl, whisk the barbecue sauce, marmalade, mustard and allspice. Pour over sausage mixture; stir to coat.
2. Cover and cook on high for 2½ to 3 hours or until heated through. Stir in pineapple. Serve with toothpicks.

Breakfast Casserole

Prep time: 15-20 minutes | Cook time: 12 hours | Serves 8

- 4 cups daikon radish
- 12 oz cooked, crumbled bacon slices
- 1 lb. cooked grounded sausage
- 1 onion, chopped
- 1 green bell pepper, sliced
- 1½ cups mushroom, sliced
- 1½ cups fresh spinach
- 2 cups shredded cheese (Monterrey Jack is preferred)
- ½ cup feta cheese, shredded
- 10 eggs
- 1 cup heavy white cream

1. First of all, put a layer of hashed browns in the bottom of the cooker with low flame.
2. Then put the layer of bacon and sausage over it.
3. Put all the spices upon the layer.
4. Now take a bowl and whisk the eggs and cream and pour the mixture in the cooker.
5. Cover it and let it cook for 6 hours on high flame or for 12 hours on low flame.

Millet Porridge with Dates

Prep time: 10 minutes | Cook time: 7 to 9 hours | Serves 4

- 1 cup cracked or whole millet
- 3 1/2 cups water
- Pinch of salt
- 1/2 cup evaporated milk, whole milk, or light cream
- 1/4 to 1/2 cup chopped pitted dates, to your taste

1. Combine the millet, water, and salt in the slow cooker. Cover and cook on LOW for 7 to 9 hours, or overnight. Stir a few times with a whisk during cooking.
2. Turn the cooker to HIGH and stir in the milk and dates; cover and cook until hot, 5 to 10 minutes.
3. Stir the porridge well and scoop into bowls with an oversized spoon. Serve with milk and honey.

Date and Nut Loaf

Prep time: 20 minutes | Cook time: 3½–4 hours | Serves 16

- 1½ cups boiling water
- 1½ cups chopped dates
- 1¼ cups sugar
- 1 egg
- 2 tsp. baking soda
- ½ tsp. salt
- 1 tsp. vanilla
- 1 tbsp. butter, melted
- 2½ cups flour
- 1 cup walnuts, chopped
- 2 cups hot water

1. Pour 1½ cups boiling water over dates. Let stand 5-10 minutes.
2. Stir in sugar, egg, baking soda, salt, vanilla, and butter.
3. In separate bowl, combine flour and nuts. Stir into date mixture.
4. Pour into 2 greased 11½-oz. coffee cans or one 8-cup baking insert. If using coffee cans, cover with foil and tie. If using baking insert, cover with its lid. Place cans or insert on rack in slow cooker. (If you don't have a rack, use rubber jar rings instead.)
5. Remove cans or insert from cooker. Let bread stand in coffee cans or baking insert 10 minutes. Turn out onto cooling rack. Slice. Spread with butter, cream cheese, or peanut butter.

Very Vanilla French Toast

Prep time: 5 minutes | Cook time: 10 minutes | Serves 4

- 1 cup whole milk
- 1 pkg. (3 oz.) cook-and-serve vanilla pudding mix
- 1 large egg
- $\frac{1}{2}$ tsp. ground cinnamon
- 8 slices texas toast
- 2 tsp. butter

1. In a large bowl, whisk the milk, pudding mix, egg and cinnamon until well blended, about 2 minutes. Dip the toast in pudding mixture, coating both sides.
2. In a large cast-iron or other heavy skillet, melt butter over medium heat. Cook bread on both sides until golden brown.

Sour Cherry & Pumpkin Seed Granola

Prep time: 10 minutes | Cook time: 5 to 6 hours on low | Serves 4 to 6

- 5 tablespoons melted coconut oil, divided
- 1 cup unsweetened shredded coconut
- 1 cup rolled oats
- 1 cup pecans
- ½ cup pumpkin seeds
- 1 ripe banana
- 1 tablespoon vanilla extract
- ½ teaspoon sea salt
- ½ teaspoon ground cinnamon
- ½ teaspoon ground ginger
- 1 cup dried sour cherries

1. Coat the slow cooker with 1 tablespoon of coconut oil.
2. In your slow cooker, toss together the coconut, oats, pecans, and pumpkin seeds.
3. In a small bowl, mash the banana with the remaining ¼ cup of melted coconut oil, the vanilla, salt, cinnamon, and ginger.
4. Add the liquid ingredients to the granola mixture and stir well to combine.
5. Cover the cooker and set to low. Cook for 5 to 6 hours (see Tip).
6. When the cooking is finished, stir in the cherries.
7. Spread the granola on a flat surface or baking sheet to cool and dry completely before storing in airtight containers. Stored in a cool place, this will keep up to six months.

Creamy Cornmeal Porridge

Prep time: 10 minutes | Cook time: 7 to 9 hours | Serves 4

- 1/2 cup coarse cornmeal, polenta, or corn grits, stone-ground if possible
- 2 cups water
- Pinch of salt
- 1/2 cup evaporated milk

1. Combine all the ingredients in the slow cooker. Cover and cook on LOW for 7 to 9 hours, or overnight. Stir a few times with a whisk or wooden spoon, if possible, during cooking.
2. Stir the porridge well and scoop into bowls with an oversized spoon. Serve with a pat of butter, milk, and a sprinkle of toasted wheat germ; or stir in cream cheese or mascarpone and top with berries.

Keto Sausage & Egg

Prep time: 15-20 minutes | Cook time: 4-5 hours | Serves 6-8

10 large eggs
10 oz pork sausage links, cooked and sliced
1 broccoli, finely chopped
1 cup cheddar shredded
¾ cup whipping cream
2 garlic cloves, minced

1. Take a 6quart ceramic slow cooker and grease its interior.
2. Put one layer of broccoli, half portion of the cheese and half part of sausage into the ceramic cooker.
3. Repeat the layering and put all the ingredients in the cooker.
4. Take a large bowl, and mix eggs, garlic, whipping cream, pepper and salt thoroughly.
5. Transfer the mix over the layered ingredients in the ceramic cooker.
6. Cover and cooker for about 5 hours.
7. Make sure the edges are not overcooked.
8. Check the center with a toothpick.

The XXL Slow Cooker Cookbook

Corn Cakes with Poached Eggs

Prep time: 30 minutes | Cook time: 15 minutes | Serves 4

Salsa:
- 3 plum tomatoes, seeded and coarsely chopped
- 1/4 cup finely chopped sweet onion
- 1/4 cup chopped sweet red pepper
- 1/4 cup chopped green pepper
- 1 tbsp. minced fresh cilantro
- 1 tbsp. lime juice
- 1 1/2 tsp. honey
- 1/2 tsp. salt
- 1/8 to 1/4 tsp. cayenne pepper
- 1/8 tsp. pepper

Corn Cakes:
- 1 can (14 3/4 oz.) cream-style corn
- 1 pkg. (6 1/2 oz.) cornbread/muffin mix
- 1/2 cup water

Eggs:
- 1 tbsp. white vinegar
- 4 large eggs

1. In a bowl, combine all salsa ingredients; let stand at room temperature while preparing corn cakes.
2. In a large bowl, mix corn, muffin mix and water. Lightly grease a griddle; heat over medium heat. Pour batter by 1/3 cupfuls onto griddle. Cook until bubbles on top begin to pop and bottoms are golden brown. Turn; cook until second side is golden brown.
3. Meanwhile, place 2-3 in. of water in a large saucepan or skillet with high sides; add white vinegar. Bring liquid to a boil; adjust heat to maintain a gentle simmer. Break cold eggs, one at a time, into a small bowl; holding bowl close to surface of water, slip egg into water.
4. Cook, uncovered, until whites are completely set and yolks begin to thicken but are not hard, 3-5 minutes Using a slotted spoon, lift eggs out of water. Serve with corn cakes and salsa.

Slow Cooker Oatmeal

Prep time: 10-15 minutes | Cook time: 8-9 hours | Serves 7-8

- 2 cups dry rolled oats
- 4 cups water
- 1 large apple, peeled and chopped
- 1 cup raisins
- 1 tsp. cinnamon
- 1-2 tbsp. orange zest

1. Combine all ingredients in your slow cooker.
2. Cover and cook on Low 8-9 hours.
3. Serve topped with brown sugar, if you wish, and milk.

Chicago-Style Beef Sandwiches

Prep time: 30 minutes | Cook time: 8 hours | Serves 12

- 1 boneless beef chuck roast (4 pounds)
- 1 teaspoon salt
- ¾ teaspoon pepper
- 2 tablespoons olive oil
- ½ pound fresh mushrooms
- 2 medium carrots, cut into chunks
- 1 medium onion, cut into wedges
- 6 garlic cloves, halved
- 2 teaspoons dried oregano
- 1 carton (32 ounces) beef broth
- 1 tablespoon beef base
- 12 Italian rolls, split
- 1 jar (16 ounces) giardiniera, drained

1. Cut roast in half; sprinkle with salt and pepper. In a large skillet, brown meat in oil on all sides. Transfer to a 5-qt. slow cooker.
2. In a food processor, combine the mushrooms, carrots, onion, garlic and oregano. Cover and process until finely chopped. Transfer to the slow cooker. Combine beef broth and base; pour over the top. Cover and cook on low for 8-10 hours or until tender.
3. Remove meat and shred with two forks. Skim fat from cooking juices. Return meat to the slow cooker; heat through. Using a slotted spoon, serve beef on buns; top with giardiniera.

Cheery Cherry Bread

Prep time: 10-15 minutes | Cook time: 2-3 hours | Serves 6-8

- 6-oz. jar maraschino cherries
- 1½ cups flour
- 1½ tsp. baking powder
- ¼ tsp. salt
- 2 eggs
- ¾ cup sugar
- ¾ cup coarsely chopped pecans

1. Drain cherries, reserving ⅓ cup syrup. Cut cherries in pieces. Set aside.
2. Combine flour, baking powder, and salt.
3. Beat eggs and sugar together until thickened.
4. Alternately add flour mixture and cherry syrup to egg mixture, mixing until well blended after each addition.
5. Fold in cherries and pecans. Spread in well greased and floured baking insert or 2-lb. coffee can. If using baking insert, cover with its lid; if using a coffee can, cover with 6 layers of paper towels. Set in slow cooker.
6. Cover cooker. Cook on High 2-3 hours.
7. Remove from slow cooker. Let stand 10 minutes before removing from pan.
8. Cool before slicing.

Cracked Wheat Porridge

Prep time: 10 minutes | **Cook time:** 7 to 9 hours | Serves 4

- 1 cup fine cracked wheat, bulgur wheat, or a 5- or 7-grain hot cereal blend
- 3 cups water
- Pinch of salt

1. Place the cracked wheat in a dry skillet and toast over medium heat until you can just smell the aroma, about 5 minutes.
2. Combine the wheat, water, and salt in the slow cooker. Cover and cook until tender on LOW for 7 to 9 hours (the cracked wheat will take longer to cook than the bulgur), or overnight, or on HIGH for 2 1/2 to 3 hours. Stir a few times with a whisk during cooking.
3. Scoop into bowls with an oversized spoon. Serve with milk and brown sugar or honey.

Bacon-Mushroom Breakfast

Prep time: 15 minutes | **Cook time:** 4 hours | Serves 4

- 3½ oz bacon large, sliced
- 2½ oz white mushrooms, chopped
- 5 eggs
- ¼ cup shallots, chopped
- ¾ cup bell pepper, chopped
- 6 kale leaves large, shredded
- 1 cup Parmesan cheese

1. Clean the kale leaves, remove the hard stems and chop into small pieces.
2. In a skillet cook the bacon, till it becomes crispy and add mushrooms, red pepper, and shallot.
3. Add kale and cut down the flame and let the kale become tender in the skillet.
4. Now take a medium bowl and beat all eggs.
5. In the slow cooker, add ghee and let it become hot.
6. Spread the ghee on all side of the cooker.
7. Put the sautéed vegetable into the base of the cooker.
8. Spread the cheese over the vegetables.
9. Then, add the beaten eggs on top.
10. Just stir it gently.
11. Set the cooker on low heat and cook for about 4 hours.
12. Serve hot with sliced avocado(optional).

Chicken-Apple Breakfast Sausage

Prep time: 15 minutes or fewer | **Cook time:** 6 to 8 hours on low | Serves 4 to 6

- 1 pound ground chicken
- ½ medium apple, peeled and minced
- 1 teaspoon sea salt
- ½ teaspoon freshly ground black pepper
- ½ teaspoon dried parsley flakes
- ½ teaspoon garlic powder
- ½ teaspoon dried basil leaves
- ¼ teaspoon ground cinnamon

1. In a large bowl, combine the chicken, apple, salt, pepper, parsley flakes, garlic powder, basil, and cinnamon. Mix well. Press the chicken mixture into the bottom of your slow cooker, ensuring it's a thin layer throughout.
2. Cover the cooker and set to low. Cook for 6 to 8 hours, or until the meat is completely cooked through.
3. Using a silicone spatula, loosen the chicken from around the edges and transfer to a cutting board. Cut into desired shapes (sticks or circles are common) and serve.

Hash Brown Pancakes with Smoked Salmon & Dill Cream

Prep time: 15 minutes | Cook time: 20 minutes | Serves 4

- ⅓ cup heavy whipping cream
- 1⅛ tsp. dill weed, divided
- 4 cups frozen shredded hash brown potatoes, thawed
- 2 large eggs, beaten
- 2 tbsp. minced chives
- ¼ tsp. salt
- 1 pkg. (3 to 4 oz.) smoked salmon or lox

1. Beat heavy whipping cream and 1 tsp. dill on high until stiff peaks form. Cover and refrigerate.
2. Preheat griddle over medium heat. Stir together the potatoes, eggs, chives and salt until well combined. Grease griddle. Drop potato mixture by heaping ½ cupfuls onto griddle; flatten to ½ in. thick.
3. Cook until the bottoms are golden brown, about 10 minutes. Turn; cook until second sides are golden brown. Keep warm.
4. To serve, place salmon slices on pancakes. Top with whipped cream; sprinkle with remaining dill.

Overnight Steel-Cut Oats

Prep time: 5 minutes | Cook time: 8 hours | Serves 4-5

- 1 cup dry steel-cut oats
- 4 cups water

1. Combine ingredients in slow cooker.
2. Cover and cook on Low overnight, or for 8 hours.
3. Stir before serving. Serve with brown sugar, ground cinnamon, fruit preserves, jam, jelly, pumpkin pie spice, fresh fruit, maple syrup, or your other favorite toppings.

Morning Millet

Prep time: 15 minutes or fewer | Cook time: 7 to 8 hours on low | Serves 4

- 1 cup millet
- 2 cups water
- 2 cups full-fat coconut milk
- ½ teaspoon sea salt
- ½ teaspoon ground cinnamon
- ½ teaspoon ground ginger
- ¼ teaspoon vanilla extract
- ½ cup fresh blueberries

1. In your slow cooker, combine the millet, water, coconut milk, salt, cinnamon, ginger, and vanilla. Stir well.
2. Cover the cooker and set to low. Cook for 7 to 8 hours.
3. Stir in the blueberries to warm at the end and serve.

Sweet Breakfast Grits

Prep time: 10 minutes | Cook time: 7 to 9 hours | Serves 4

- 1/2 cup corn grits, stone-ground if possible
- 2 cups water
- Pinch of salt
- 3 tablespoons honey or pure maple syrup
- Sliced fruit or berries for serving

1. Combine the grits, water, and salt in the slow cooker. Cover and cook on LOW for 7 to 9 hours, or overnight.
2. Stir the grits a few times during cooking with a whisk and stir in the honey just before serving. Stir well and scoop into bowls with an oversized spoon. Serve with milk and sliced fruit or berries.

Egg & Mushroom Breakfast

Prep time: 15 minutes | Cook time: 6 hours | Serves 4

- 1 cup mushrooms, chopped
- 3 large slices of bacon
- 6 eggs
- 3 tbsp shallots, chopped
- ½ cup bell pepper, red
- 8 large kale leaves, shredded
- 1 cup Parmesan cheese, shredded
- 1 tbsp butter or ghee
- ¼ tbsp pepper
- salt to taste
- spinach - for dressing
- avocado, sliced - for dressing
- extra virgin olive oil - for dressing

1. Wash, clean and slice the bacon.
2. Wash, clean and remove the stem of the kale and chop it nicely.
3. Take a pan and cook bacon until it becomes crispy.
4. Add mushroom, pepper, and shallot and continue heating until it becomes soft.
5. Now add kale and switch off the stove and let the kale wilt.
6. Take a small mixing bowl and beat the eggs, with pepper and salt.
7. Put on the slow cooker and add some butter.
8. Grease the inside of the cooker properly with the butter.
9. Transfer the sautéed vegetables to the cooker.
10. Spread the cheese over it.
11. Add the beaten egg on top of the mixture.
12. Stir well and slow heat about 6 hours.
13. You may occasionally check the food after 4 hours.
14. Serve it with sliced avocado, spread with spinach dressed in olive oil.

Breakfast Oatmeal

Prep time: 5 minutes | Cook time: 8 hours | Serves 6

- 2 cups dry rolled oats
- 4 cups water
- 1 tsp. salt

1. Combine all ingredients in slow cooker.
2. Cover and cook on Low overnight, or for 8 hours.

Banana Loaf

Prep time: 5-10 minutes | Cook time: 2-2½ hours | Serves 6-8

- 3 very ripe bananas
- ½ cup butter, softened
- 2 eggs
- 1 tsp. vanilla
- 1 cup sugar
- 1 cup flour
- 1 tsp. baking soda

1. Combine all ingredients in an electric mixing bowl. Beat 2 minutes or until well blended. Pour into well greased 2-lb. coffee can.
2. Place can in slow cooker. Cover can with 6 layers of paper towels between cooker lid and bread.
3. Cover cooker. Bake on High 2-2½ hours, or until toothpick inserted in center comes out clean. Cool 15 minutes before removing from pan.

Caramel-Apple Oats

Prep time: 15 minutes or fewer | Cook time: 6 to 8 hours on low | Serves 4

- 1 tablespoon coconut oil
- 3 sweet apples, such as fuji or gala, peeled and sliced
- 2 tablespoons coconut sugar
- ¼ teaspoon sea salt
- 1 teaspoon ground ginger
- 1 teaspoon ground cinnamon
- 1 teaspoon vanilla extract
- 2 cups rolled oats
- 1 cup unsweetened applesauce
- 3 cups unsweetened almond milk
- ½ cup water

1. Coat the slow cooker with the coconut oil.
2. Layer the sliced apples along the bottom of the slow cooker so each piece is touching the bottom.
3. In this order, layer in the coconut sugar, salt, ginger, cinnamon, vanilla, oats, applesauce, almond milk, and water.
4. Cover the cooker and set to low. Cook for 6 to 8 hours and serve.

Vegetarian Stew in Bread Bowls

Prep time: 30 minutes | Cook time: 8 ½ hours | Serves 10

- 3 cups cubed red potatoes (about 4 medium)
- 2 cups chopped celery (about 4 ribs)
- 2 medium leeks (white portion only), cut into ½-inch pieces
- 1 ¾ cups coarsely chopped peeled parsnips (about 2 medium)
- 1 ½ cups chopped carrots (about 3 medium)
- 1 can (28 ounces) Italian crushed tomatoes
- 1 can (14 ½ ounces) vegetable broth
- 2 teaspoons sugar
- ½ teaspoon salt
- ½ teaspoon dried thyme
- ½ teaspoon dried rosemary, crushed
- 3 tablespoons cornstarch
- 3 tablespoons cold water
- 10 round loaves sourdough bread (8 to 9 ounces each)

1. In a 4- or 5-qt. slow cooker, combine the first 1Cook, covered, on low 8-9 hours or until vegetables are tender.
2. In a small bowl, mix the cornstarch and water until smooth. Stir into stew. Cook, covered, on high 30 minutes or until thickened.
3. Cut a thin slice off the top of each bread loaf. Hollow out the bottoms of the loaves, leaving ½-in.-thick shells (save removed bread for another use). Serve stew in bread bowls.

Golden Beet & Spinach Frittata

Prep time: 15 minutes or fewer | Cook time: 5 to 7 hours on low | Serves 4 to 6

- 1 tablespoon extra-virgin olive oil
- 8 large eggs
- 1 cup packed fresh spinach leaves, chopped
- 1 cup diced peeled golden beets
- ½ medium onion, diced
- ¼ cup unsweetened almond milk
- ¾ teaspoon sea salt
- ½ teaspoon garlic powder
- ½ teaspoon dried basil leaves
- freshly ground black pepper

1. Coat the slow cooker with the olive oil.
2. Cover the cooker and set to low. Cook for 5 to 7 hours, or until the eggs are completely set, and serve.

Chapter 4

Poultry

Pork and Green Chili Stew

Prep time: 40 minutes | Cook time: 7 hours | Serves 8

- 2 pounds boneless pork shoulder butt roast, cut into 3/4-inch cubes
- 1 large onion, cut into $\frac{1}{2}$-in. pieces
- 2 tablespoons canola oil
- 1 teaspoon salt
- 1 teaspoon coarsely ground pepper
- 4 large potatoes, peeled and cut into $\frac{3}{4}$-inch cubes
- 3 cups water
- 1 can (16 ounces) hominy, rinsed and drained
- 2 cans (4 ounces each) chopped green chilies
- 2 tablespoons quick-cooking tapioca
- 2 garlic cloves, minced
- $\frac{1}{2}$ teaspoon dried oregano
- $\frac{1}{2}$ teaspoon ground cumin
- 1 cup minced fresh cilantro
- sour cream, optional

1. In a large skillet, brown pork and onion in oil in batches. Sprinkle with salt and pepper. Transfer to a 4-qt. slow cooker.
2. Stir in the potatoes, water, hominy, chilies, tapioca, garlic, oregano and cumin. Cover and cook on low for 7-9 hours or until meat is tender, stirring in cilantro during the last 30 minutes of cooking. Serve with sour cream if desired.

Chicken Tortilla Casserole

Prep time: 25 minutes | Cook time: 3-6 hours | Serves 8-10

- 4 whole boneless, skinless chicken breasts, cooked and cut in 1-inch pieces (reserve ¼ cup broth chicken was cooked in)
- 10 6-inch flour tortillas, cut in strips about ½-inch wide × 2-inches long
- 2 medium onions, chopped
- 1 tsp. canola oil
- 10¾-oz. can fat-free chicken broth
- 10¾-oz. can 98% fat-free cream of mushroom soup
- 2 4-oz. cans mild green chilies, chopped
- 1 egg
- 1 cup shredded low-fat cheddar cheese

1. Pour reserved chicken broth in slow cooker sprayed with non-fat cooking spray.
2. Scatter half the tortilla strips in bottom of slow cooker.
3. Mix remaining ingredients together, except the second half of the tortilla strips and the cheese.
4. Layer half the chicken mixture into the cooker, followed by the other half of the tortillas, followed by the rest of the chicken mix.
5. Cover. Cook on Low 4-6 hours, or on High 3-5 hours.
6. Add the cheese to the top of the dish during the last 20-30 minutes of cooking.
7. Uncover and allow casserole to rest 15 minutes before serving.

Savory Slow Cooker Chicken

Prep time: 10-15 minutes | Cook time: 8-10 hours | Serves 4

- 2½ lbs. chicken pieces, skinned
- 1 lb. fresh tomatoes, chopped, **or** 15-oz. can stewed tomatoes
- 2 tbsp. white wine
- 1 bay leaf
- ¼ tsp. pepper
- 2 garlic cloves, minced
- 1 onion, chopped
- ½ cup chicken broth
- 1 tsp. dried thyme
- 1½ tsp. salt
- 2 cups broccoli, cut into bite-sized pieces

1. Combine all ingredients except broccoli in slow cooker.
2. Cover. Cook on Low 8-10 hours.
3. Add broccoli 30 minutes before serving.

Mandarin Turkey Tenderloin

Prep time: 15 minutes | Cook time: 4 ½ hours | Serves 8

- 8 turkey breast tenderloins (4 ounces each)
- ½ teaspoon ground ginger
- ½ teaspoon crushed red pepper flakes
- 1 can (11 ounces) mandarin oranges, drained
- 1 cup sesame ginger marinade
- ½ cup chicken broth
- 1 package (16 ounces) frozen stir-fry vegetable blend, thawed
- 1 tablespoon sesame seeds, toasted
- 1 green onion, sliced
- hot cooked rice, optional

1. Place the turkey in a 3-qt. slow cooker. Sprinkle with ginger and red pepper flakes. Top with oranges. In a small bowl, combine marinade and broth; pour over turkey.
2. Cover and cook on low for 4-5 hours or until a thermometer reads 170°.
3. Stir the vegetables into the slow cooker. Cover and cook 30 minutes longer or until the vegetables are heated through.
4. Sprinkle with sesame seeds and green onion. Serve with rice if desired.

Lemony Herbs Chicken

Prep time: 10 minutes | Cook time: 4 hours | Serves 4

- 18 oz chicken breasts, skinless, boneless, and cut into pieces
- 3/4 cup chicken broth
- 2 tbsp olive oil
- 2 tbsp butter
- 3 tbsp lemon juice
- 1/8 tsp dried thyme
- 1/4 tsp dried basil
- 1 tsp dried oregano
- 1 tsp dried parsley
- 3 tbsp rice flour

1. In a bowl, toss chicken with rice flour.
2. Add butter and olive oil in a cooking pot and set instant pot aura on sauté mode.
3. Add chicken to the cooking pot and cook until brown.
4. Add remaining ingredients on top of the chicken.
5. Cover instant pot aura with lid.
6. Select slow cook mode and cook on Low for 4 hours.
7. Serve and enjoy.

The XXL Slow Cooker Cookbook | 27

Salsa Turkey Loaf

Prep time: 10 minutes | Cook time: 3 hours | Serves 6

Sauce
- 2 tablespoons olive oil
- 2 medium onions, coarsely chopped
- 2 medium red bell peppers, seeded and coarsely chopped
- 1 Anaheim chile, seeded and coarsely chopped
- 1 teaspoon ground cumin
- ½ teaspoon dried oregano
- ¼ teaspoon ancho chile powder
- One 28- to 32-ounce can tomato purée
- 1½ teaspoons salt

Meat Loaf
- Four 6-inch flour tortillas, coarsely chopped
- ¼ cup milk
- 2 pounds ground turkey
- ½ cup finely chopped onion
- 1 clove garlic, minced
- ¼ cup finely chopped fresh cilantro
- ¼ cup prepared mild salsa
- 1 large egg, beaten
- 1 teaspoon salt

1. Heat the oil in a sauté pan over medium-high heat. Add the onions, bell peppers, chile, cumin, oregano, and chile powder and sauté until the vegetables are softened, 5 to 7 minutes. Add the tomato purée and salt to the pan and stir to combine.
2. Transfer the contents of the skillet to the insert of a 5- to 7-quart slow cooker. Cover and cook on low while making the meat loaf.
3. Soak the tortillas in the milk in a large mixing bowl for 5 minutes, breaking them up with a fork.
4. Add the remaining ingredients and stir to combine. Form the mixture into a 3-inch-wide by 8-inch-long loaf. Place the loaf on top of the sauce in the slow-cooker insert and spoon some of the sauce over it.
5. Cover and cook on high for 3 hours, until the meat loaf is cooked through and registers 175°F on an instant-read thermometer. Skim off any fat from the surface of the sauce. Carefully remove the meat loaf from the sauce, cover with aluminum foil, and allow it to rest for 15 minutes.
6. Slice the meat loaf and serve with the sauce on the side.

Queso Chicken Tacos

Prep time: 10 minutes | Cook time: 4 hours | Serves 8

- 2 lb. chicken breasts, boneless & skinless
- 1 1/2 cups Mexican cheese dip
- 10 oz can Rotel
- 1 oz taco seasoning

1. Add all ingredients into the cooking pot and stir well.
2. Cover instant pot aura with lid.
3. Select slow cook mode and cook on Low for 4-6 hours.
4. Remove chicken from pot and shred using a fork, return shredded chicken to the pot and stir well.
5. Serve and enjoy.

Asian Meatballs

Prep time: 10 minutes | Cook time: 3 hours | Serves 6

Sauce

- 1 cup soy sauce
- 2/3 cup rice wine (mirin) or dry sherry
- 2 cups chicken broth
- ½ cup white miso
- 1 clove garlic, sliced
- 2 dime-size slices fresh ginger

Meat Balls

- 1 pound ground turkey
- 1 pound lean ground pork
- 2 teaspoons freshly grated ginger
- 1 clove garlic, minced
- 4 green onions, finely chopped, plus additional for garnish
- 1 large egg white, beaten
- ½ teaspoon hot sauce
- 2 tablespoons cornstarch mixed with
- ¼ cup water or chicken broth
- Sesame seeds for garnish

1. Put all the sauce ingredients in the insert of a 5- to 7-quart slow cooker and stir to combine.
2. Cover and cook on high while preparing the meatballs.
3. Combine all the meatball ingredients in a large bowl and stir. Roll the mixture into 2-inch balls and place in the slowcooker insert.
4. Cover and cook on high for 3 hours, until the meatballs are cooked through and register 175°F on an instant-read thermometer.
5. Remove the meatballs from the sauce and transfer the sauce to a saucepan. Bring the sauce to a boil, add the cornstarch mixture, and bring back to a boil.
6. Serve the sauce with the meatballs, and garnish with the additional green onions and sesame seeds.

Garlic Herb Roasted Pepper Chicken

Prep time: 10 minutes | Cook time: 4 hours | Serves 6

- 2 lb. chicken thighs, skinless and boneless
- 1 cup roasted red peppers, chopped
- 1/2 cup chicken or vegetable stock
- 1 cup olives
- 1 tsp dried thyme
- 1 tsp oregano
- 1 tbsp capers
- 3 garlic cloves, minced
- 1 onion, sliced
- 1 tbsp olive oil

1. Add all ingredients into the cooking pot and stir well.
2. Cover instant pot aura with lid.
3. Select slow cook mode and cook on Low for 4 hours.
4. Stir well and serve.

Slow Cook Turkey Breast

Prep time: 10 minutes | Cook time: 4 hours 30 minutes | Serves 6

- 4 lb. turkey breast
- 2 tbsp fresh lemon juice
- 1/2 cup sun-dried tomatoes, chopped
- 1/2 cup olives, chopped
- 3 tbsp flour
- 3/4 cup chicken stock
- 3 garlic cloves, chopped
- 1 tsp dried oregano
- 1 onion, chopped

1. Add turkey breast, garlic, oregano, lemon juice, sun-dried tomatoes, olives, onion, pepper, and salt to the cooking pot.
2. Pour half stock over turkey.
3. Cover instant pot aura with lid.
4. Select slow cook mode and cook on Low for 4 hours.
5. Whisk together remaining stock and flour and add into the cooking pot and stir well, cover, and cook on Low for 30 minutes more.
6. Serve and enjoy.

Chili-Lime Chicken Tostadas

Prep time: 10 minutes | Cook time: 5 hours | Serves 5

- 4 pounds bone-in chicken breast halves, skin removed
- 1 medium onion, chopped
- 1 can (4 ounces) chopped green chilies
- 3 tablespoons lime juice
- 4 1/2 teaspoons chili powder
- 4 garlic cloves, minced
- 10 tostada shells
- 1 can (16 ounces) fat-free refried beans

Optional:
- shredded cabbage, shredded cheddar cheese, salsa, sour cream, sliced ripe olives and guacamole

1. In a 4-qt. slow cooker, combine chicken and onion. In a small bowl, combine the green chilies, lime juice, chili powder and garlic; pour over chicken. Cover and cook on low for 5-6 hours or until meat is tender.
2. Remove chicken; cool slightly. Set aside $2/3$ cup cooking juices. Discard remaining juices. Shred chicken with two forks and return to slow cooker. Stir in reserved cooking juices.
3. Spread tostadas with refried beans; top with chicken. Layer with cabbage, cheese, salsa, sour cream, olives and guacamole if desired.

Tandoori Chicken Panini

Prep time: 25 minutes | Cook time: 3 hours | Serves 6

- 1 1/2 lbs. boneless skinless chicken breasts
- 1/4 cup reduced-sodium chicken broth
- 2 garlic cloves, minced
- 2 tsp. minced fresh gingerroot
- 1 tsp. paprika
- 1/4 tsp. salt
- 1/4 to 1/2 tsp. cayenne pepper
- 1/4 tsp. ground turmeric
- 6 green onions, chopped
- 6 tbsp. chutney
- 6 naan flatbreads

1. Place first eight ingredients in a 3-qt. slow cooker. Cook, covered, on low until chicken is tender, 3-4 hours.
2. Shred chicken with two forks. Stir in the green onions.
3. Cook sandwiches on a panini maker or indoor grill until golden brown, 6-8 minutes. To serve, cut each sandwich in half.

Creamy Chicken Curry

Prep time: 10 minutes | Cook time: 6 hours | Serves 6

- 1 ½ lb. chicken thighs, boneless
- ½ cup chicken broth
- 3 potatoes, peeled and cut into 1-inch pieces
- 10 oz can coconut milk
- 2 tbsp brown sugar
- ½ tsp red pepper, crushed
- ½ tsp coriander, crushed
- 3 tbsp curry powder
- 3 tbsp fresh ginger, chopped

1. Add all ingredients into the cooking pot and stir well.
2. Cover instant pot aura with lid.
3. Select slow cook mode and cook on Low for 6 hours.
4. Stir well and serve.

Parmesan Chicken Rice

Prep time: 10 minutes | Cook time: 4 hours | Serves 6

- 4 chicken breasts, skinless & boneless
- ¼ cup parmesan cheese, grated
- 1 cup of rice
- 2 cup milk
- 20 oz can cream of chicken soup

1. Season chicken with pepper and salt and place into the cooking pot.
2. Mix together rice, milk, and soup and pour over chicken and top with parmesan cheese.
3. Cover instant pot aura with lid.
4. Select slow cook mode and cook on High for 4 hours.
5. Remove chicken from pot and chop, return chicken to the pot and stir well.
6. Serve and enjoy.

Chicken and Bean Torta

Prep time: 20 minutes | Cook time: 4-5 hours | Serves 6

1 lb. uncooked boneless, skinless chicken breasts
1 medium onion
½ tsp. garlic salt
¼ tsp. black pepper
15-oz. can ranch-style black beans
15-oz. can low-sodium diced tomatoes with green chilies
4 tortillas
1½ cups shredded low-fat cheddar cheese
salsa
fat-free sour cream
lettuce
tomatoes

1. Cut chicken in small pieces. Brown with onion in nonstick skillet. Drain well.
2. Season with garlic salt and pepper. Stir in beans and tomatoes.
3. Place strips of foil on bottom and up sides of slow cooker, forming an X. Spray foil and cooker lightly with non-fat cooking spray.
4. Place 1 tortilla on bottom of cooker. Spoon on one-third of chicken mixture and one-quarter of the cheese.
5. Repeat layers, ending with a tortilla sprinkled with cheese on top.
6. Cover. Cook on Low 4-5 hours.
7. Serve with salsa, sour cream, lettuce, and tomatoes.

The XXL Slow Cooker Cookbook | 31

Red-Cooked Chicken

Prep time: 10 minutes | **Cook time:** 2 hours | Serves 4

Red-Cooking Liquid:
- 1 1/2 cups water
- 1 cup soy sauce
- 1/4 cup rice wine or dry sherry
- 2 tablespoons sugar
- 2 green onions (white and green parts), roughly chopped
- Two 1/2-inch slices ginger, lightly crushed
- 1 whole star anise (see Note)
- One 4-inch cinnamon stick
- 1 clove garlic, lightly crushed
- 1 strip (about 3 inches) orange zest, removed with a vegetable peeler

1. Remove the chicken giblets and neck and reserve for another use. Cut off any lumps of fat. If you have time, place the chicken on a plate and refrigerate it uncovered for a couple of hours. The drier the chicken is, the more color it will absorb from the sauce.
2. Combine the red-cooking liquid ingredients in the slow cooker and stir to dissolve the sugar. Add the chicken and turn to coat it with liquid. Leave it breast side up. Cover and cook on HIGH for 1 hour.
3. Carefully turn the chicken over, breast side down, using a sturdy wooden spoon inserted in the cavity and a rubber spatula to help you guide the chicken; take care to avoid splashing. Cover and cook on HIGH until an instant-read thermometer inserted into the thickest part of the thigh registers 180°F, about 1 hour more.
4. Remove the chicken from the cooker. If you wish to serve it cold, refrigerate, uncovered, until chilled before cutting it up. To serve the chicken warm, put it on a cutting board and allow it to cool a bit. Then carve the chicken Western style, or if you have a heavy cleaver, chop it into 2-inch pieces. Arrange the chicken on a platter and drizzle a few tablespoons of the cooking liquid over it.
5. Allow the cooking liquid to cool a bit, then pour it through a strainer into a heavy glass jar. Discard any solids. Refrigerate the liquid, but do not cap the jar until the liquid has cooled completely. It will keep in the refrigerator for a week to 10 days. For longer storage between uses, freeze it. Thaw before cooking with it. To reuse the red-cooking liquid, discard the solidified fat at the top. Pour the liquid into the cooker, add a fresh chicken, and proceed as directed in the recipe. After every third or fourth use, refresh the liquid by adding 1/2 cup of soy sauce and half of the seasonings.

Chicken Curry

Prep time: 10 minutes | Cook time: 4 to 4 1/2 hours | Serves 4

- 2 to 3 pounds mixed boneless chicken breast halves and thighs, breast halves each cut into 2 pieces
- 3 tablespoons sesame or olive oil
- 3 medium-size onions, chopped
- 2 cloves garlic, pressed; or 2 jalapeño chiles, seeded and chopped
- 1 1/2 teaspoons ground coriander
- 1 teaspoon ground turmeric
- 1 teaspoon ground cumin
- 1 tablespoon chopped fresh ginger
- 2 teaspoons paprika
- 1/2 teaspoon red pepper flakes
- 1/2 teaspoon brown mustard seeds
- One 28-ounce can crushed tomatoes
- Juice of 1/2 lemon
- 1 head cauliflower, broken into small florets, stems discarded
- 1 cup frozen petite peas, thawed; or 2 to 3 cups fresh baby spinach
- Salt to taste

1. Cut the chicken thighs into large or small pieces, removing the skin (leave the skin on the breast pieces). Coat the slow cooker with nonstick cooking spray. Heat the oil in a large skillet over medium-high heat and brown the chicken on all sides; transfer to a plate. Add the onions to the pan and cook, stirring a few times, until softened, about 5 minutes. Add the garlic or chiles, coriander, turmeric, cumin, ginger, paprika, red pepper flakes, and mustard seeds and cook gently for 2 minutes, stirring constantly. Add the tomatoes and lemon juice and mix well. Purée half of the tomato-onion mixture in a blender or food processor or in the pan with a handheld immersion blender.
2. In layers, add to the cooker one-third of the chicken (dark meat first) and one-quarter of the sauce, and sprinkle with one-third of the cauliflower. Repeat the layers two more times, and finish with the remainder of the sauce. Cover and cook on HIGH for 1 hour.
3. Turn the cooker to LOW and cook for 4 to 4 1/2 hours.
4. During the last 30 minutes, toss in some peas or a few handfuls of fresh baby spinach, season with the salt, cover, and cook until tender. To cook a bit faster, switch to HIGH heat.

Bavarian Pot Roast

Prep time: 10 minutes | Cook time: 7 hours | Serves 6

- 1 beef top round roast (2 pounds)
- 1 cup unsweetened apple juice
- 1/2 cup tomato sauce
- 1 small onion, chopped
- 1 tablespoon white vinegar
- 1 1/2 teaspoons minced fresh gingerroot
- 1 teaspoon salt
- 1 teaspoon ground cinnamon
- 2 tablespoons cornstarch
- 1/4 cup water

1. In a large skillet coated with cooking spray, brown roast on all sides. Transfer to a 3-qt. slow cooker.
2. In a small bowl, combine the juice, tomato sauce, onion, vinegar, ginger, salt and cinnamon; pour over roast. Cover and cook on low for 6 hours.
3. In a small bowl, combine the cornstarch and water until smooth; stir into the cooking juices until well combined.
4. Cover and cook 1 hour longer or until the meat is tender and the gravy begins to thicken.

Simple Chicken & Mushrooms

Prep time: 10 minutes | Cook time: 6 hours | Serves 2

- 2 chicken breasts, skinless and boneless
- 1 cup mushrooms, sliced
- ½ tsp thyme, dried
- 2 onion, sliced
- 1 cup chicken stock

1. Add all ingredients into the cooking pot and stir well.
2. Cover instant pot aura with lid.
3. Select slow cook mode and cook on Low for 6 hours.
4. Stir well and serve.

Easy Mexican Chicken

Prep time: 10 minutes | Cook time: 6 hours | Serves 6

- 2 lb. chicken breasts, boneless & skinless
- 1/3 cup chicken stock
- 1 oz taco seasoning
- 2 cups salsa

1. Add all ingredients into the cooking pot and stir well.
2. Cover instant pot Aura with lid.
3. Select slow cook mode and cook on Low for 6 hours.
4. Remove chicken from pot and shred using a fork, return shredded chicken to the pot and stir well.
5. Serve and enjoy.

Southwest Chicken

Prep time: 15 minutes | Cook time: 4 hours | Serves 6

- 1 can (15 1/4 ounces) whole kernel corn, drained
- 1 can (15 ounces) black beans, rinsed and drained
- 1 jar (16 ounces) mild salsa
- 4 boneless skinless chicken breast halves (5 ounces each)
- sweet red and yellow pepper strips, sour cream, shredded cheddar cheese and sliced green onions, optional

1. In a 3-qt. slow cooker, layer three-fourths each of the corn and beans and half of the salsa. Arrange chicken over salsa; top with remaining corn, beans and salsa. Cover and cook on low for 4-5 hours or until chicken is tender.
2. Shred chicken with two forks and return to the slow cooker; heat through. Top with the peppers, sour cream, cheese and onions if desired.

34 | The XXL Slow Cooker Cookbook

Chicken-Vegetable Dish

Prep time: 10 minutes | Cook time: 2-5 hours | Serves 4

- 4 skinless bone-in chicken breast halves
- 15-oz. can crushed tomatoes
- 10-oz. pkg. frozen green beans
- 2 cups water **or** chicken broth
- 1 cup brown rice, uncooked
- 1 cup sliced mushrooms
- 2 carrots, chopped
- 1 onion, chopped
- ½ tsp. minced garlic
- ½ tsp. herb-blend seasoning
- ¼ tsp. dried tarragon

1. Combine all ingredients in slow cooker.
2. Cover. Cook on High 2 hours, and then on Low 3-5 hours.

Mango & Grilled Chicken Salad

Prep time: 20 minutes | Cook time: 25 minutes | Serves 4

- 1 lb. chicken tenderloins
- ½ tsp. salt
- ¼ tsp. pepper

Salad:
- 6 cups torn mixed salad greens
- ¼ cup raspberry or balsamic vinaigrette
- 1 medium mango, peeled and cubed
- 1 cup fresh sugar snap peas, halved lengthwise

1. Toss chicken tenderloins with salt and pepper. Moisten a paper towel with cooking oil; using long-handled tongs, rub on grill rack to coat lightly.
2. Grill chicken, covered, over medium heat or broil 4 in. from heat until no longer pink, 3-4 minutes on each side. Cut chicken into 1-in. pieces.
3. Divide greens among four plates; drizzle with vinaigrette. Top with chicken, mango and peas; serve immediately.

Chinese Poached Chicken

Prep time: 10 minutes | Cook time: 6 to 7 hours | Serves 4

One 3- to 4-pound broiler/fryer
1 bunch green onions (white and green parts), trimmed
2 cloves garlic, bruised
5 coin-sized slices ginger, peeled and bruised with the side of a large knife
1/2 cup fresh cilantro sprigs
1 whole star anise
1/4 cup light soy sauce
3 tablespoons dry vermouth
1/4 cup water

1. Remove the chicken giblets and neck and reserve for another use. Cut off any lumps of fat. Put the green onions, garlic, ginger, cilantro, and anise in the cavity. Put the chicken in the slow cooker, breast side up. Combine the soy sauce, vermouth, and water in a small bowl and pour over the chicken. Cover and cook on LOW until an instant-read thermometer inserted in the thickest part of the thigh registers 180°F, 6 to 7 hours.
2. Transfer the chicken to a platter. Pour the liquid from the cooker into a separate container and refrigerate; then skim off the fat after it congeals. Or pour the cooking juices into a gravy separator and then into a container and refrigerate if not using. When the chicken is cool enough to handle, remove the skin, and cut or shred the meat from the carcass. Refrigerate the meat if not using it immediately.

Rosemary Lemon Wings

Prep time: 10 minutes | Cook time: 3 hours | Serves 8

- 3 pounds chicken wing drumettes
- ¼ cup olive oil
- 1½ teaspoons salt
- 1 teaspoon sweet paprika
- Freshly ground black pepper

Sauce

- ½ cup lemon juice
- Grated zest of 3 lemons
- 2 teaspoons salt
- Pinch of red pepper flakes
- ½ cup extra-virgin olive oil
- 2 tablespoons red wine vinegar
- 6 cloves garlic, minced
- 1 tablespoon finely minced fresh rosemary
- ½ cup chicken broth

1. Coat the insert of a 5- to 7-quart slow cooker with nonstick cooking spray. Preheat the broiler for 10 minutes.
2. Combine the wings, olive oil, salt, paprika, and a generous grinding of pepper in a large mixing bowl and toss until the wings are evenly coated. Arrange the wings on a wire rack in a baking sheet and broil until the wings are crispy on one side, about 5 minutes.
3. Turn the wings and broil until crispy and browned an additional 5 minutes.
4. Remove the wings from the oven. If you would like to do this step ahead of time, cool the wings and refrigerate for up to 2 days. Otherwise, put the wings in the prepared cooker insert.
5. Combine all the sauce ingredients in a mixing bowl and stir. Pour the sauce over the wings and turn to coat.
6. Cover and cook on high for 3 hours, turning the wings several times to coat with the sauce.
7. Serve the wings from the cooker set on warm.

Cape Breton Chicken

Prep time: 15 minutes | Cook time: 7 hours | Serves 5

- 4 boneless, skinless chicken breast halves, uncooked, cubed
- 1 medium onion, chopped
- 1 medium green bell pepper, chopped
- 1 cup chopped celery
- 1 quart low-sodium stewed **or** crushed tomatoes
- 1 cup water
- ½ cup tomato paste
- 2 tbsp. Worcestershire sauce
- 2 tbsp. brown sugar
- 1 tsp. black pepper

1. Combine all ingredients in slow cooker.
2. Cover. Cook on Low 7 hours.
3. Serve over rice.

Chicken Soft Tacos

Prep time: 5 minutes | Cook time: 6-8 hours | Serves 6

- 1-1½ lbs. frozen, boneless, skinless chicken breasts
- 14½-oz. can low-sodium diced tomatoes with green chilies
- 1 envelope low-sodium taco seasoning

1. Place chicken breasts in slow cooker.
2. Mix tomatoes and taco seasoning. Pour over chicken.
3. Cover. Cook on Low 6-8 hours.
4. Serve in soft tortillas. Top with salsa, low-fat shredded cheddar cheese, guacamole if your diet allows, and fresh tomatoes.

Chapter 5

Beef, Pork and Lamb

Chicago-Style Italian Beef

Prep time: 10 minutes | Cook time: 8 hours | Serves 8

- Three 1½- to 2-pound flanks steaks
- 4 cloves garlic
- 1 teaspoon dried oregano
- 1 teaspoon dried basil
- 1 bay leaf
- 2 shallots, coarsely chopped
- ½ cup soy sauce
- ½ cup red wine vinegar
- ½ teaspoon freshly ground black pepper
- ¼ cup extra-virgin olive oil
- 4 large onions, cut into half rounds
- 2 medium green bell peppers, seeded and thinly sliced
- 2 medium red bell peppers, seeded and thinly sliced
- Two 15-ounce cans double-strength beef broth
- 8 crusty rolls (see savvy)

1. Put the flank steaks into a 2-gallon zipper-top plastic bag. Mix the garlic, oregano, basil, bay leaf, shallots, soy sauce, vinegar, pepper, and 2 tablespoons of the oil together in a bowl. Pour the marinade into the bag and toss with the meat to coat. Seal the bag and refrigerate for at least 6 hours or overnight.
2. Remove the meat from the marinade and discard the marinade. Roll the steaks from the short side and place them in the bottom of the insert of a 5- to 7-quart slow cooker. Heat the remaining oil in a large skillet over medium-high heat. Add the onions and sauté until they are softened and begin to turn translucent, 5 to 7 minutes. Add the bell peppers and sauté until they are softened, about 5 minutes.
3. Transfer the onions and bell peppers to the cooker and stir in the broth. Cover and cook on low for 8 hours, until the meat is tender.
4. Serve the meat, onions, and peppers from the cooker along with the crusty rolls.

Java Roast Beef

Prep time: 10 minutes | Cook time: 8 hours | Serves 12

- 5 garlic cloves, minced
- 1½ teaspoons salt
- ¾ teaspoon pepper
- 1 boneless beef chuck roast (3 to 3½ pounds)
- 1½ cups strong brewed coffee
- 2 tablespoons cornstarch
- ¼ cup cold water

1. Combine the garlic, salt and pepper; rub over beef. Transfer to a 4-qt. slow cooker. Pour coffee around meat. Cover and cook on low for 8-10 hours or until meat is tender. Remove meat to a serving platter; keep warm.
2. Skim fat from cooking juices; transfer to a small saucepan. Bring to a boil. Combine cornstarch and water until smooth; gradually stir into the pan. Bring to a boil; cook and stir for 2 minutes or until thickened. Serve with meat.

Beer-Braised Stew

Prep time: 20 minutes | Cook time: 6 hours | Serves 8

- 3 bacon strips, diced
- 2 pounds beef stew meat, cut into 1-inch cubes
- 1/2 teaspoon pepper
- 1/4 teaspoon salt
- 2 tablespoons canola oil
- 2 cups fresh baby carrots
- 1 medium onion, cut into wedges
- 1 teaspoon minced garlic
- 1 bay leaf
- 1 can (12 ounces) beer or nonalcoholic beer
- 1 tablespoon soy sauce
- 1 tablespoon Worcestershire sauce
- 1 teaspoon dried thyme
- 2 tablespoons all-purpose flour
- 1/4 cup water
- hot cooked noodles

1. In a large skillet, cook bacon over medium heat until crisp. Remove to paper towels; drain, discarding drippings. Sprinkle beef with pepper and salt. In the same skillet, brown beef in oil in batches; drain.
2. Transfer to a 5-qt. slow cooker. Add the carrots, bacon, onion, garlic and bay leaf. In a small bowl, combine the beer, soy sauce, Worcestershire sauce and thyme. Pour over beef mixture.
3. Cover and cook on low for 5 1/2 to 6 hours or until meat and vegetables are tender.
4. In a small bowl, combine flour and water until smooth. Gradually stir into slow cooker. Cover and cook on high for 30 minutes or until thickened. Discard bay leaf. Serve beef with noodles.

Beef and Artichokes Bowls

Prep time: 10 minutes | Cook time: 7 hours | Serves 2

- 1 lb. beef sirloin, chopped
- 1 tsp cayenne pepper
- 1 tsp white pepper
- 4 artichoke hearts, chopped
- 1 cup of water

1. Mix meat with white pepper and cayenne pepper.
2. Transfer it in the slow cooker bowl.
3. Add salt, artichoke hearts, and water.
4. Close the lid and cook the meal on Low for 7 hours.

Sweet and Spicy Jerk Ribs

Prep time: 10 minutes | Cook time: 6 hours | Serves 5

- 4 1/2 pounds pork baby back ribs
- 3 tablespoons olive oil
- 1/3 cup Caribbean jerk seasoning
- 3 cups honey barbecue sauce
- 3 tablespoons apricot preserves
- 2 tablespoons honey

1. Cut ribs into serving-size pieces; brush with oil and rub with jerk seasoning. Place in a 5- or 6-qt. slow cooker. Combine the remaining; pour over ribs.
2. Cover and cook on low for 6-8 hours or until meat is tender. Skim fat from sauce before serving.

The XXL Slow Cooker Cookbook | 39

Easy Meatball Stroganoff

Prep time: 30 minutes | Cook time: 30 minutes | Serves 4

- 3 cups uncooked egg noodles
- 1 tbsp. olive oil
- 1 pkg. (12 oz.) frozen fully cooked italian meatballs, thawed
- 1 1/2 cups beef broth
- 1 tsp. dried parsley flakes
- 3/4 tsp. dried basil
- 1/2 tsp. salt
- 1/2 tsp. dried oregano
- 1/4 tsp. pepper
- 1 cup heavy whipping cream
- 3/4 cup sour cream

1. Cook egg noodles according to package directions for al dente; drain.
2. Meanwhile, in a large skillet, heat oil over medium-high heat. Brown meatballs; remove from pan. Add broth, stirring to loosen the browned bits from pan. Add the seasonings. Bring to a boil; cook until liquid is reduced to 1/2 cup, 5-7 minutes.
3. Add meatballs, noodles and cream. Bring to a boil. Reduce heat; simmer, covered, until slightly thickened, 3-5 minutes. Stir in sour cream; heat through.

Salsa Beef Fajitas

Prep time: 10 minutes | Cook time: 8 to 10 hours | Serves 8

- 4 cups prepared salsa
- 1½ teaspoons ground cumin
- ¼ cup freshly squeezed lime juice
- Two 1½-pound flank steaks

1. Combine the salsa, cumin, and lime juice in the insert of a 5- to 7-quart slow cooker. Roll the flank steaks from the short side and place in the slow cooker.
2. Cover and cook on low for 8 to 10 hours, until the meat is tender. Remove the meat from the sauce, allow it to rest for 15 minutes, and shred, using two forks.
3. Skim off any fat from the top of the sauce and return the meat to the slow cooker. Stir to blend with the sauce.
4. Serve the meat directly from the cooker.

Fruited Flank Steak

Prep time: 5 minutes | Cook time: 7-9 hours | Serves 5

- 1 lb. flank steak
- ¼ tsp. salt
- dash of black pepper
- 30-oz. can fruit cocktail in light syrup
- 1 tbsp. vegetable oil
- 1 tbsp. lemon juice
- ¼ cup low-sodium teriyaki sauce
- 1 tsp. red wine vinegar
- 1 clove garlic, minced

1. Place flank steak in slow cooker. Sprinkle with salt and pepper.
2. Drain fruit cocktail, saving ¼ cup syrup.
3. Combine ¼ cup syrup with remaining ingredients, except fruit.
4. Pour syrup over steak.
5. Cover. Cook on Low 7-9 hours.
6. Add drained fruit during the last 10 minutes of cooking time.
7. Cut meat into thin slices across the grain to serve.

Beef and Scallions Bowl

Prep time: 10 minutes | Cook time: 5 hours | Serves 4

- 1 lb. beef stew meat, cubed
- 1 tsp chili powder
- 1 cup corn kernels, frozen
- 1 cup of water
- 2 tbsp tomato paste
- 2 tsp minced garlic

1. Mix water with tomato paste and pour the liquid in the slow cooker.
2. Add chili powder, beef, corn kernels, and minced garlic Close the lid and cook the meal on high for 5 hours.
3. When the meal is cooked, transfer the mixture in the bowls and top with scallions.

Balsamic Beef

Prep time: 15 minutes | Cook time: 9 hours | Serves 4

- 1 lb. beef stew meat, cubed
- 1 tsp cayenne pepper
- 2 tbsp balsamic vinegar
- ½ cup of water
- 2 tbsp butter

1. Toss the butter in the skillet and melt it.
2. Then add meat and roast it for 2 minutes per side on medium heat.
3. Transfer the meat with butter in the slow cooker.
4. Add balsamic vinegar, cayenne pepper, and water.
5. Close the lid and cook the meal on Low for 9 hours.

Barbacoa Lamb

Prep time: 5 minutes | Cook time: 6 hours | Serves 2

- ¼ cup dried mustard
- 5 ½ lb. lamb leg, boneless
- 2 tbsp. smoked paprika
- 2 tbsp. Himalayan salt
- 1 tbsp. chipotle powder
- 1 tbsp. dried oregano
- 1 tbsp. ground cumin
- 1 cup water

1. Combine the paprika, oregano, chipotle powder, cumin, and salt.
2. Cover the roast with the dried mustard and sprinkle with the prepared spices. Arrange the lamb in the slow cooker, cover the cooker with the lid and let the lamb marinate in the refrigerator overnight.
3. In the morning, let the lamb come to room temperature. Once you're ready to cook, just add the cup of water to the slow cooker. Cook on High for 6 hours.
4. When done, remove all except for one cup of the cooking juices, then shred the lamb.
5. Using the rest of the cooking juices, adjust the seasoning as you desire. Serve

Pork Tenderloin Braised In Milk with Fresh Herbs

Prep time: 10 minutes | **Cook time:** 5 to 6 1/2 hours | **Serves 4**

- 1/4 cup olive oil
- 2 1/2 pounds pork tenderloin, trimmed of fat and silver skin and blotted dry
- 1 tablespoon minced fresh oregano
- 1 tablespoon minced fresh tarragon
- 2 teaspoons minced fresh rosemary
- 1 3/4 teaspoons salt
- 8 grinds of black pepper
- 2 to 2 1/4 cups hot whole milk

1. In a large skillet over medium-high heat, heat the oil until very hot. Add the meat and cook until browned on all sides, 4 to 5 minutes total. Transfer to the slow cooker. Sprinkle with the herbs, salt, and pepper. Add the milk; it should come halfway up the sides of the pork. Cover and cook on LOW until the pork is fork-tender, 5 to 6 1/2 hours.
2. Transfer the pork to a warm platter and let rest for 10 minutes. Cut the roast into 1/2-inch-thick slices and spoon over the creamy, thick sauce.

Pacific Rim Braised Short Ribs

Prep time: 10 minutes | **Cook time:** 8 hours | **Serves 4–6**

- 1½ tablespoons vegetable oil
- ½ cup firmly packed light brown sugar
- 4½ pounds boneless short ribs, fat trimmed (see savvy)
- ½ teaspoon freshly ground black pepper
- 4 cups sliced sweet onions, such as Vidalia or red onions (about 4 medium to large)
- 6 cloves garlic, minced
- 1 teaspoon freshly grated ginger
- 2 tablespoons hoisin sauce
- ½ cup soy sauce
- 1½ cups chicken broth
- Chopped green onions for garnishing
- Toasted sesame seeds for garnishing

1. Heat the oil in a large skillet over medium-high heat. Pat half the brown sugar onto the ribs. Add the ribs a few at a time to the skillet and brown on all sides, being careful not to burn the sugar.
2. Transfer the ribs to the insert of a 5- to 7-quart slow cooker. Add the onions, garlic, and ginger to the skillet over mediumhigh heat and sauté until the onions and garlic are fragrant, about 4 minutes.
3. Transfer the contents of the skillet to the slow-cooker insert and stir in the remaining sugar, the hoisin, soy sauce, and broth. Sprinkle with the pepper. Cover the slow cooker and cook on high for 8 hours or on low for 3½ to 4 hours, until the meat is tender.
4. Remove the meat from the slow-cooker insert. Skim off any fat from the sauce and pour some of the sauce over the meat. Serve any remaining sauce on the side. Garnish the ribs with the green onions and sesame seeds.

Cheeseburger Skillet Dinner

Prep time: 20 minutes | Cook time: 25 minutes | Serves 6

- 1 pkg. (7 1/4 oz.) macaroni and cheese
- 1 lb. ground turkey or beef
- 1/2 cup chopped onion
- 1 pkg. (16 oz.) frozen mixed vegetables
- 1/3 cup ketchup
- 1/4 cup water
- 1/2 tsp. prepared mustard
- 1/4 tsp. garlic powder
- 3/4 cup shredded cheddar cheese
- salt and pepper to taste

1. Prepare macaroni and cheese according to package directions.
2. Meanwhile, in a large skillet, brown the turkey or beef with the onion; drain. Stir in the vegetables, ketchup, water, mustard and garlic powder.
3. Cook until the vegetables are crisp-tender, about 10 minutes. Add cheddar cheese and stir until melted. Mix in macaroni and cheese. Season with salt and pepper.

Mahogany Glazed Pork

Prep time: 10 minutes | Cook time: 8 to 10 hours | Serves 4

- 1/3 cup soy sauce
- 1/2 cup orange marmalade
- 1 to 2 cloves garlic, to your taste, pressed
- 1 to 1 1/2 teaspoons red pepper flakes, to your taste
- 3 tablespoons ketchup
- One 3 1/2-pound boneless Boston pork butt, cut into large pieces, or 3 1/2 pounds country-style pork spareribs
- 8 ounces sugar snap peas
- 1/2 cup julienned red bell pepper

1. Coat the slow cooker with nonstick cooking spray.
2. Combine the soy sauce, marmalade, garlic, red pepper flakes, and ketchup in a small bowl and mix until smooth; brush over both sides of the meat. Arrange the pork butt or ribs in the cooker. (If you have a round cooker, stack the ribs.) Pour over any extra sauce. Cover and cook on LOW until fork-tender and the meat starts to separate from the bone, 8 to 10 hours.
3. Stir in the sugar snap peas and bell pepper; cover and let stand a few minutes to warm. Serve immediately.

Mustard Beef

Prep time: 10 minutes | Cook time: 8 hours | Serves 4

- 1 lb. beef sirloin, chopped
- 1 tbsp capers, drained
- 1 cup of water
- 2 tbsp mustard
- 2 tbsp coconut oil

1. Mix meat with mustard and leave for 10 minutes to marinate.
2. Then melt the coconut oil in the skillet.
3. Add meat and roast it for 1 minute per side on high heat.
4. After this, transfer the meat in the slow cooker.
5. Add water and capers.
6. Cook the meal on Low for 8 hours.

Lamb with Mint and Green Beans

Prep time: 8 minutes | Cook time: 10 hours | Serves 2

- ½ tsp. Himalayan pink salt
- black pepper, freshly ground, to taste
- 1 lamb leg, bone-in
- 2 tbsp. lard/ghee/tallow
- 4 garlic cloves
- 6 cups trimmed green beans
- ¼ mint, freshly chopped/1–2 tbsp. dried mint

1. Heat the slow cooker.
2. Dry the lamb with some paper towels. Sprinkle with pepper and salt. Grease a Dutch oven or a similar large pot with ghee/lard.
3. Sear the lamb until golden brown and then set it aside.
4. Peel and mince the garlic. Dice up the mint. Arrange the seared meat into the slow cooker and give it a shake with the garlic and mint.
5. Cover the slow cooker with the lid and cook on low for 10 hours.
6. After about 4 hours, take the lamb out of the cooker. Toss it into the green beans and then return the lamb to the slow cooker. (You can add ½–1 cup of water to the cooker if it gets dried out.)
7. Let the flavors mingle for about 2 hours. (The meat should be tender and the beans crispy.) Serve and enjoy!

Slow-Cooked Pork and Beans

Prep time: 15 minutes | Cook time: 6 hours | Serves 12

- 1 boneless pork loin roast (3 pounds)
- 1 medium onion, sliced
- 3 cans (15 ounces each) pork and beans
- 1½ cups barbecue sauce
- ¼ cup packed brown sugar
- 1 teaspoon garlic powder

1. Cut roast in half; place in a 5-qt. slow cooker. Top with onion. In a large bowl, combine the beans, barbecue sauce, brown sugar and garlic powder; pour over meat. Cover and cook on low for 6-8 hours or until meat is tender.
2. Remove roast; shred with two forks. Return meat to slow cooker; heat through.

Cilantro Beef

Prep time: 10 minutes | Cook time: 4.5 hours | Serves 4

- 1 lb. beef loin, roughly chopped
- ¼ cup apple cider vinegar
- 1 tbsp dried cilantro
- 1 tsp dried basil
- 1 cup of water
- 2 tsp tomato paste

1. Mix meat with tomato paste, dried cilantro, and basil.
2. Then transfer it in the slow cooker.
3. Add apple cider vinegar and water.
4. Cook the cilantro beef for 4.5 hours on High.

Tender Texas-Style Steaks

Prep time: 5 minutes | Cook time: 6 hours | Serves 4-6

- steaks **or** chops
- 1 cup brown sugar
- 1 cup ketchup
- salt to taste
- pepper to taste
- few dashes of Worcestershire sauce

1. Lay steaks in bottom of slow cooker.
2. Combine sugar and ketchup. Pour over steaks.
3. Sprinkle with salt and pepper and a few dashes of Worcestershire sauce.
4. Cover. Cook on High 3 hours then on Low 3 hours.
5. Serve with wide egg noodles, green beans, and applesauce. Spoon some of the juice from the cooker over the noodles. Thicken the juice if you like with a little flour.

Breaded Pork Tenderloin

Prep time: 30 minutes | Cook time: 30 minutes | Serves 4

- 1 pork tenderloin (1 lb.)
- $1/3$ cup all-purpose flour
- $1/3$ cup cornbread/muffin mix
- $1/2$ tsp. salt
- $1/4$ tsp. pepper
- 1 large egg, beaten
- 4 tbsp. canola oil
- ranch or barbecue sauce, optional

1. Cut pork crosswise into $1/2$-in. slices. In a shallow bowl, mix flour, muffin mix, salt and pepper. Place egg in a separate shallow bowl. Dip pork in egg, then in flour mixture, patting to help coating adhere.
2. In a large skillet, heat 2 tbsp. oil over medium heat. Add half of the pork; cook until a thermometer reads 145°, 3-4 minutes on each side. Drain on paper towels. Wipe skillet clean; repeat with remaining oil and pork. If desired, serve with sauce.

Succulent Lamb

Prep time: 15 minutes | Cook time: 8 hours | Serves 2

- ¼ cup olive oil
- 1 (2-lb.) lamb leg
- 1 tbsp. maple syrup
- 2 tbsp. whole grain mustard
- 4 thyme sprigs
- 6–7 mint leaves
- ¾ tsp. dried rosemary
- ¾ tsp. garlic
- pepper and salt, to taste

1. Cut the string/netting off the lamb. Slice 3 slits on the lamb.
2. Cover the meat with the oil and the rub (mustard, pepper, salt, and maple syrup). Push the rosemary and garlic into the slits.
3. Place the lamb in the slow cooker and cook on low for 7 hours. Garnish with mint and thyme. Cook for 1 hour more. Then transfer onto a platter and serve.

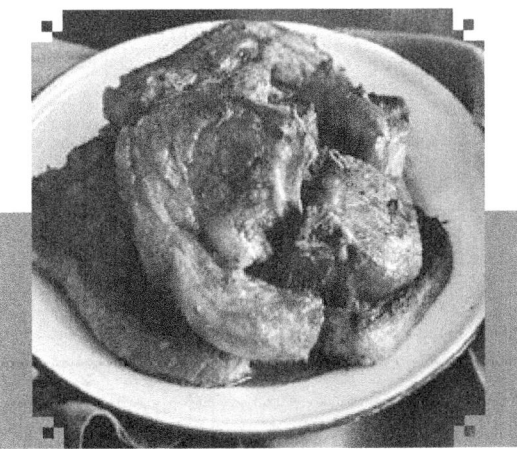

The XXL Slow Cooker Cookbook

Pub-Crawl Short Ribs

Prep time: 10 minutes | Cook time: 3½ to 4 hours | Serves 4–6

- Salt and freshly ground black pepper
- ¼ cup Colman's English mustard or Stonewall Kitchen Pub Style mustard (see savvy)
- 4½ pounds boneless short ribs, fat trimmed
- 1½ tablespoons canola oil
- 4 cups coarsely chopped sweet onions, such as Vidalia
- 2 teaspoons dried thyme
- 2 cups baby carrots
- 2 cups peeled parsnips, cut into chunks
- 1 tablespoon prepared horseradish
- 1 cup Guinness stout
- 1 cup double-strength beef broth
- 2 tablespoons unsalted butter, at room temperature (optional)
- 2 tablespoons all-purpose flour (optional)

1. Mix 1½ teaspoons salt, ½ teaspoon pepper, and the mustard together in a small bowl. Rub the mixture over the short ribs and allow the ribs to sit at room temperature for about 15 minutes.
2. Heat the oil in a large skillet over high heat. Add the ribs a few at a time and brown on all sides. Transfer to the insert of a 5- to 7-quart slow cooker.
3. Add the onions and thyme to the same skillet over mediumhigh heat and sauté until the onions are softened and fragrant. Transfer the onions to the slow cooker and stir in the carrots, parsnips, horseradish, stout, and broth.
4. Cover the slow cooker and cook on low for 8 hours or on high for 3½ to 4 hours. Remove the meat and vegetables from the pan, cover with aluminum foil, and allow to rest for 15 minutes. If you would like a smooth sauce, strain it through a fine-mesh sieve. Skim off any fat from the sauce and season with salt and pepper.
5. Serve the ribs and vegetables with the sauce. Serve immediately.

Pork Chops with Tomato Sauce and Mushrooms

Prep time: 10 minutes | Cook time: 6 to 8 hours | Serves 4

- 4 thick bone-in pork loin chops, at least 1 inch thick, blotted dry
- 8 ounces mushrooms, sliced
- 1 medium-size yellow onion, chopped
- 1 large red or yellow bell pepper, seeded and cut into rings or strips
- 1 clove garlic, minced
- Two 8-ounce cans tomato sauce
- 2 tablespoons balsamic vinegar
- 2 tablespoons minced fresh flat-leaf parsley
- 1/2 teaspoon dried oregano
- 1/2 teaspoon dried basil
- Pinch of salt
- 2 tablespoons cornstarch
- 1/4 cup cold water

1. 1. In a large, heavy skillet over medium-high heat, brown the pork chops on both sides.
2. In the slow cooker, combine the mushrooms, onion, bell pepper, and garlic. Nestle the pork chops on top.
3. In a medium-size bowl, combine the tomato sauce, vinegar, parsley, oregano, basil, and salt. Pour over the pork chops. Cover and cook on LOW until the meat is tender, 6 to 8 hours.
4. Transfer the pork to a platter and tent with aluminum foil to keep warm. Transfer the tomato sauce to a medium-size saucepan. In a small bowl, whisk together the cornstarch and water until smooth, and stir the slurry into the sauce. Bring to a boil over medium heat, stirring, until slightly thickened, about 2 minutes. Serve the sauce over the pork chops.

Onion Beef

Prep time: 10 minutes | Cook time: 5.5 hours | Serves 14

- 4 lb. beef sirloin, sliced
- 2 cup white onion, chopped
- 1 cup of water
- ½ cup butter
- 1 bay leaf

1. Mix beef sirloin with salt and ground black pepper and transfer in the slow cooker.
2. Add butter, water, onion, and bay leaf.
3. Close the lid and cook the meat on High for 5.5 hours.

Cranberry-Ginger Pork Ribs

Prep time: 20 minutes | Cook time: 5 hours | Serves 8

- 1 can (14 ounces) whole-berry cranberry sauce
- 2 habanero peppers, seeded and minced
- 4 ½ teaspoons minced grated gingerroot
- 3 garlic cloves, minced
- 2 ½ pounds boneless country-style pork ribs
- ½ teaspoon salt
- ½ teaspoon cayenne pepper
- ½ teaspoon pepper
- 2 tablespoons olive oil
- hot cooked rice

1. In a small bowl, combine cranberry sauce, habanero peppers, ginger and garlic. Sprinkle the ribs with salt and peppers. In a large skillet, brown ribs in oil on all sides; drain.
2. Transfer meat to a 3-qt. slow cooker; pour berry mixture over ribs. Cover and cook on low for 5-6 hours or until meat is tender.
3. Skim fat from cooking juices. Serve with pork and rice.

Slow Cooker Sauerbraten

Prep time: 20 minutes | Cook time: 6 hours | Serves 10

- 1 boneless beef chuck roast or rump roast (3 to 4 pounds)
- 4 cups water
- 1 bottle (14 ounces) ketchup
- 1 large onion, chopped
- ¾ cup packed brown sugar
- ¾ cup cider vinegar
- 1 tablespoon mixed pickling spices
- 3 bay leaves
- 1 ½ cups crushed gingersnap cookies (about 30 cookies)

Gravy:
- 2 tablespoons cornstarch
- ¼ cup cold water

1. Cut the roast in half. Place in a 5-qt. slow cooker; add the water. In a large bowl, combine the ketchup, onion, brown sugar and cider vinegar; pour over the roast.
2. Place mixed pickling spices and bay leaves on a double thickness of cheesecloth; bring up the corners of the cheesecloth and tie with string to form a spice bag. Add the spice bag and gingersnap cookie crumbs to the slow cooker.
3. Cover and cook on low for 6-8 hours or until meat is tender.
4. Remove the roast and keep warm. Discard the spice bag. Strain the cooking juices; transfer 4 cups to a large saucepan.
5. Combine cornstarch and water until smooth; stir into the cooking juices. Bring to a boil; cook and stir for 2 minutes or until thickened. Slice roast; serve with gravy.

Chapter 6

Fish and Seafood

Chicken and Shrimp Casserole

Prep time: 15-20 minutes | Cook time: 3-8 hours | Serves 6

- 1¼ cups rice, uncooked
- 2 tbsp. butter, melted
- 3 cups fat-free, low-sodium chicken broth
- 1 cup water
- 3 cups cut-up, cooked skinless chicken breast
- 2 4-oz. cans sliced mushrooms, drained
- ⅓ cup light soy sauce
- 12-oz. pkg. shelled frozen shrimp
- 8 green onions, chopped, 2 tbsp. reserved
- ⅔ cup slivered almonds

1. Combine rice and butter in slow cooker. Stir to coat rice well.
2. Add remaining ingredients except almonds and 2 tbsp. green onions.
3. Cover. Cook on Low 6-8 hours, or on High 3-4 hours, until rice is tender.
4. Sprinkle almonds and green onions over top before serving.

Shrimp Creole

Prep time: 30 minutes | Cook time: 6-8 hours | Serves 8-10

- ½ cup butter
- ⅓ cup flour
- 1¾ cups sliced onions
- 1 cup diced green peppers
- 1 cup diced celery
- 1½ large carrots, shredded
- 2¾-lb. can tomatoes
- ¾ cup water
- ½ tsp. dried thyme
- 1 garlic clove, minced
- pinch of rosemary
- 1 tbsp. sugar
- 3 bay leaves
- 1 tbsp. Worcestershire sauce
- 1 tbsp. salt
- ⅛ tsp. dried oregano
- 2 lbs. shelled shrimp, deveined

1. Melt butter in skillet. Add flour and brown, stirring constantly. Add onions, green peppers, celery, and carrots. Cook 5-10 minutes. Transfer to slow cooker.
2. Add remaining ingredients, except shrimp, and stir well.
3. Cover. Cook on Low 6-8 hours.
4. Add shrimp during last hour.
5. Serve over rice.

Poached Salmon in Court-Bouillon Recipe

Prep time: 5 minutes | Cook time: 2 hours 30 minutes | Serves 2

- 2 whole black peppercorns
- 1 medium carrot, thinly sliced
- 1/2 celery rib, thinly sliced
- 2 salmon steaks in 1-inch-thick slices
- 1 tbsp white wine vinegar

1. Put all the items in the slow cooker except for the salmon.
2. You can also add parsley and bay leaf for extra flavor.
3. Rub salmon slices with salt and pepper to taste.
4. Cook within 2 hours on high.
5. Put some of the liquid over the top.
6. Cook again within 30 minutes, high.

Soy-Ginger Steamed Pompano

Prep time: 5 minutes | Cook time: 1 hour | Serves 4

- 1 wild-caught whole pompano, gutted and scaled
- 1 bunch scallion, diced
- 1 bunch cilantro, chopped
- 3 teaspoons minced garlic
- 1 tbsp. grated ginger
- 1 tbsp. swerve sweetener
- ¼ cup soy sauce
- ¼ cup white wine
- ¼ cup sesame oil

1. Place scallions in a 6-quart slow cooker and top with fish.
2. Whisk together the remaining ingredients, except for cilantro, and pour the mixture all over the fish.
3. Plug in the slow cooker, shut with lid and cook for 1 hour at High heat setting or until cooked through.
4. Garnish with cilantro and serve.

Beantown Scallops

Prep time: 10 minutes | Cook time: 4 hours | Serves 6

- 1 cup (2 sticks) unsalted butter
- 2 tablespoons olive oil
- 2 cloves garlic, minced
- 2 teaspoons sweet paprika
- ¼ cup dry sherry
- 2 pounds dry-pack sea scallops (see savvy)
- ½ cup finely chopped fresh Italian parsley

1. Put the butter, oil, garlic, paprika, and sherry in the insert of a 5- to 7-quart slower cooker.
2. Cover and cook on low for 4 hours. Turn the cooker to high and add the scallops, tossing them in the butter sauce. Cover and cook on high for 30 to 40 minutes, until the scallops are opaque.
3. Transfer the scallops and sauce from the slow cooker to a serving platter. Sprinkle with the parsley and serve.

Garlic Shrimp

Prep time: 5 minutes | Cook time: 1 hour | Serves 5

For the Garlic Shrimp:
- 1 1/2 lb. large wild-caught shrimp, peeled and deveined
- 1/8 tsp ground cayenne pepper
- 2 ½ tsp minced garlic
- 1/4 cup avocado oil
- 4 tbsp unsalted butter

For the Seasoning:
- 1 tsp onion powder
- 1 tbsp garlic powder
- 1 tbsp paprika
- 1 tsp dried oregano
- 1 tsp dried thyme

1. Stir together all the ingredients for seasoning, garlic, oil, and butter and add to a 4-quart slow cooker.
2. Plugin the slow cooker, shut with lid, and cook for 25 to 30 minutes at high heat setting or until cooked.
3. When done, transfer shrimps to a serving plate, top with sauce, and serve.

50 | The XXL Slow Cooker Cookbook

Salmon Poached in White Wine

Prep time: 15 minutes | Cook time: 2 hours | Serves 4

- 2.2 lb. salmon fillet, skin on
- 2 cups of water
- 1 cup cooking white wine
- 1 lemon, sliced thin
- 1 small mild onion, sliced thin
- 1 bay leaf
- 1 mixed bunch fresh tarragon, dill, and parsley

1. Add all fixings, except salmon and seasoning, to the slow cooker.
2. Cover, cook on low for 1 hour.
3. Season the salmon, place in the slow cooker skin-side down.
4. Cover, cook on low for another hour.
5. Serve.

Shrimp Marinara

Prep time: 15 minutes | Cook time: 6¼-7¼ hours | Serves 6

- 16-oz. can low-sodium tomatoes, cut up
- 2 tbsp. minced parsley
- 1 clove garlic, minced
- ½ tsp. dried basil
- ½ tsp. salt
- ¼ tsp. black pepper
- 1 tsp. dried oregano
- 6-oz. can tomato paste
- ½ tsp. seasoned salt
- 1 lb. shrimp, cooked and shelled
- 3 cups spaghetti
- grated Parmesan cheese

1. Combine tomatoes, parsley, garlic, basil, salt, pepper, oregano, tomato paste, and seasoned salt in slow cooker.
2. Cover. Cook on Low 6-7 hours.
3. Stir shrimp into sauce.
4. Cover. Cook on Low 10-15 minutes.
5. Serve over cooked spaghetti. Top with Parmesan cheese.

Southwestern Fish Tacos

Prep time: 20 minutes | Cook time: 30 minutes | Serves 2

- ¼ cup mayonnaise
- ¼ cup sour cream
- 2 tbsp. minced fresh cilantro
- 4 tsp. taco seasoning
- ½ lb. cod or haddock fillets, cut into 1-in. pieces
- 1 tbsp. lemon juice
- 1 tbsp. canola oil
- 4 taco shells
- optional ingredients: shredded lettuce, chopped tomato and lime wedges

1. For sauce, mix mayonnaise, sour cream, cilantro and 2 tsp. taco seasoning. In another bowl, toss the cod with lemon juice and the remaining taco seasoning.
2. In a skillet, heat oil over medium-high heat; saute cod just until it begins to flake easily with a fork, 4-6 minutes (fish may break apart as it cooks).
3. Spoon into taco shells; serve with sauce and remaining ingredients as desired.

Clam Chowder

Prep time: 5 minutes | Cook time: 6 hours | Serves 6

- 20-ounce wild-caught baby clams, with juice
- ½ cup chopped scallion
- ½ cup chopped celery
- 1 teaspoon salt
- 1 teaspoon ground black pepper
- 1 teaspoon dried thyme
- 1 tbsp. avocado oil
- 2 cups coconut cream, full-fat
- 2 cups chicken broth

1. Grease a 6-quart slow cooker with oil, then add ingredients and stir until mixed.
2. Plug in the slow cooker, shut with lid and cook for 4 to 6 hours at Low heat setting or until cooked through.
3. Serve immediately.

Chicken and Shrimp Jambalaya

Prep time: 15 minutes | Cook time: 2¼-3¾ hours | Serves 5-6

- 3½-4-lb. roasting chicken, cut up
- 3 onions, diced
- 1 carrot, sliced
- 3-4 garlic cloves, minced
- 1 tsp. dried oregano
- 1 tsp. dried basil
- 1 tsp. salt
- ⅛ tsp. white pepper
- 14-oz. can crushed tomatoes
- 1 lb. shelled raw shrimp
- 2 cups rice, cooked

1. Combine all ingredients except shrimp and rice in slow cooker.
2. Cover. Cook on Low 2-3½ hours, or until chicken is tender.
3. Add shrimp and rice.
4. Cover. Cook on High 15-20 minutes, or until shrimp are done.

Company Seafood Pasta

Prep time: 15 minutes | Cook time: 1-2 hours | Serves 4-6

- 2 cups sour cream
- 3 cups shredded Monterey Jack cheese
- 2 tbsp. butter, melted
- ½ lb. crabmeat **or** imitation flaked crabmeat
- ⅛ tsp. pepper
- ½ lb. bay scallops, lightly cooked
- 1 lb. medium shrimp, cooked and peeled

1. Combine sour cream, cheese, and butter in slow cooker.
2. Stir in remaining ingredients.
3. Cover. Cook on Low 1-2 hours.
4. Serve immediately over linguine. Garnish with fresh parsley.

The XXL Slow Cooker Cookbook

Soy Steamed Pompano

Prep time: 5 minutes | Cook time: 1 hour | Serves 4

- 1 wild-caught whole pompano, gutted and scaled
- 1 bunch scallion, diced
- 1 bunch cilantro, chopped
- 3 tsp minced garlic
- 1 tbsp grated ginger
- 1 tbsp swerve sweetener
- ¼ cup of soy sauce
- ¼ cup white wine
- ¼ cup sesame oil

1. Place scallions in a 6-quart slow cooker and top with fish.
2. Whisk together remaining ingredients, except for cilantro, and pour the mixture all over the fish.
3. Plugin the slow cooker, shut with lid, and cook for 1 hour at high heat or until cooked.
4. Garnish with cilantro and serve.

Vietnamese Braised Catfish

Prep time: 5 minutes | Cook time: 6 hours | Serves 3

- 1 fillet of wild-caught catfish, cut into bite-size pieces
- 1 scallion, chopped
- 3 red chilies, chopped
- 1 tbsp. grated ginger
- 1/2 cup swerve sweetener
- 2 tbsp. avocado oil
- 1/4 cup fish sauce, unsweetened

1. Place a small saucepan over medium heat, add sweetener and cook until it melts.
2. Then add scallion, chilies, ginger, and fish sauce and stir until mixed.
3. Transfer this mixture to a 4-quart slow cooker, add fish and toss until coated.
4. Plug in the slow cooker, and shut with lid, and cook for 6 hours at Low heat setting until it is cooked.
5. Drizzle with avocado oil and Serve immediately.

Vietnamese Catfish

Prep time: 5 minutes | Cook time: 6 hours | Serves 3

- 1 fillet of wild-caught catfish, cut into bite-size pieces
- 2 scallion, chopped
- 2 red chilies, chopped
- 1 tbsp grated ginger
- 1/2 cup swerve sweetener
- 3 tbsp avocado oil
- 1/4 cup fish sauce, unsweetened

1. Put a small saucepan over medium heat, put the sweetener, and cook until it melts.
2. Then add scallion, chilies, ginger, and fish sauce and stir until mixed.
3. Transfer this mixture in a 4-quart slow cooker, add fish and toss until coated.
4. Plugin the slow cooker, shut with lid, and cook for 6 hours at low heat setting until cooked.
5. Drizzle with avocado oil and serve straight away.

The XXL Slow Cooker Cookbook | 53

Chili Shrimps

Prep time: 15 minutes | Cook time: 2 hours | Serves 6

- 1 lb. peeled and deveined raw shrimps
- 1 lb. tomatoes, fire-roasted
- 2 tbsp spicy salsa
- ½ cup chopped bell pepper
- ½ tsp cumin
- ½ tsp cayenne pepper
- ½ tsp minced garlic
- 2 tbsp chopped cilantro
- 2 tbsp olive oil

1. Drizzle the slow cooker with a generous amount of olive oil.
2. Place the shrimps at the bottom of it.
3. Put the rest of the fixing into the slow cooker.
4. Cook on high for 2 hours.

Spicy Shrimps

Prep time: 10 minutes | Cook time: 3 hours | Serves 2

- ¼ lb. shrimp, shelled and deveined
- 1 tsp olive oil
- 1 onion, diced
- 5 cloves of garlic, minced
- 1 tsp red pepper flakes
- 1 can fire-roasted tomatoes
- 1 tbsp Italian parsley

1. Set the slow cooker to high heat and heat the oil.
2. Sauté the onion and garlic for 2 minutes.
3. Add the pepper flakes and tomatoes—season with black pepper and salt.
4. Add the shrimps.
5. Adjust the heat setting to low and cook for 2 or 3 hours.
6. Garnish with parsley.

Garlic Crab Claws

Prep time: 10 minutes | Cook time: 5½ hours | Serves 6–8

- 1 cup (2 sticks) unsalted butter
- ½ cup olive oil
- 10 cloves garlic, sliced (see savvy)
- 2 tablespoons Old Bay seasoning
- 2 cups dry white wine or vermouth
- 1 lemon, thinly sliced
- 3 to 4 pounds cooked crab legs and claws, cracked (see savvy)

1. Put the butter, oil, garlic, seasoning, wine, and lemon in the insert of a 5- to 7-quart slow cooker.
2. Cover and cook on low for 4 hours. Add the crab, spoon the sauce over the crab, and cook for an additional 1½ hours, turning the crab in the sauce during cooking.
3. Serve the crab from the cooker set on warm.

Braised Squid with Tomatoes and Fennel

Prep time: 20 minutes | Cook time: 4 hours | Serves 2

- 1 1/2 cups clam juice
- 1 can plum tomatoes
- 1/2 fennel bulb, minced
- 4 tbsp all-purpose flour
- 1 lb. squid in 1-inch pieces

1. Add chopped onions, fennel, and garlic to the flameproof insert of a slow cooker and cook on a stove in medium heat for about 5 minutes.
2. Transfer to the slow cooker, cover, and cook for 3 hours on low.
3. Uncover, add the squid and mix well—Cook for another 1 hour.

Lemon Pepper Tilapia

Prep time: 5 minutes | Cook time: 3 hours | Serves 6

- 6 wild-caught Tilapia fillets
- 4 teaspoons lemon-pepper seasoning, divided
- 6 tbsp. unsalted butter, divided
- 1/2 cup lemon juice, fresh

1. Cut a large piece of aluminum foil for each fillet and then arrange them in a clean working space.
2. Place each fillet in the middle of the foil, then season with lemon-pepper seasoning, drizzle with lemon juice, and top with 1 tbsp. butter.
3. Gently crimp the edges of foil to form a packet and place it into a 6-quart slow cooker.
4. Plug in the slow cooker, shut with lid and cook for 3 hours at High heat setting or until cooked through.
5. When done, carefully remove packets from the slow cooker and open the crimped edges and check the fish, it should be tender and flaky.
6. Serve immediately.

Crab Cioppino

Prep time: 10 minutes | Cook time: 4 to 6 hour | Serves 4

- 1/4 cup olive oil
- 1 medium-size yellow onion, finely chopped
- 2 cloves garlic, minced
- One 15-ounce can tomato sauce
- Two 28-ounce cans whole plum tomatoes, drained a bit (if packed in purée, don't drain)
- 1 cup dry white wine
- 1 bay leaf
- 1 tablespoon dried basil, or 3 tablespoons chopped fresh basil
- 1 teaspoon red pepper flakes
- 1/2 teaspoon dried oregano
- Salt and freshly ground black pepper to taste
- 3 steamed whole crabs, cracked and cleaned (ask your fishmonger to do this)

1. In a medium-size skillet, heat the oil over medium heat, then cook the onion, stirring, until softened, about 5 minutes. Add the garlic and cook, stirring, for 2 minutes. Transfer to the slow cooker and add the tomato sauce, tomatoes, wine, bay leaf, basil, pepper flakes, and oregano. Break up the tomatoes with the back of a spoon. Cover and simmer on LOW for 4 to 6 hours.
2. Season with salt and pepper. Add the crab, cover, and cook on HIGH for 20 to 30 minutes to heat the crab through. Serve immediately.
1. Mixed Seafood Cioppino: In place of the crabs, substitute 1 pound of medium-size (16 to 20 count) shrimp with their tails left on, peeled and deveined; 2 cracked and cleaned steamed crabs; 1/2 pound large sea scallops; and 1 pound white-fleshed fish fillets, such as red snapper, sea bass, halibut, or monkfish. Add to the hot tomato sauce during the last 20 to 30 minutes of cooking.

Garlic Salmon Linguine

Prep time: 20 minutes | Cook time: 30 minutes | Serves 6

- 1 pkg. (16 oz.) linguine
- 1/3 cup olive oil
- 3 garlic cloves, minced
- 1 can (14 3/4 oz.) salmon, drained, bones and skin removed
- 3/4 cup chicken broth
- 1/4 cup minced fresh parsley
- 1/2 tsp. salt
- 1/8 tsp. cayenne pepper

1. Cook linguine according to the package directions; drain.
2. Meanwhile, in a large skillet, heat oil over medium heat. Add garlic; cook and stir until tender, about 1 minute (do not allow to brown).
3. Stir in the remaining ingredients; heat through. Add the linguine; toss gently to combine.

Shrimp Creole Stew

Prep time: 10 minutes | Cook time: 5 to 6 hours | Serves 4

- One 14.5-ounce can diced tomatoes, with their juice
- One 14.5-ounce can chicken broth
- 1 1/2 cups chopped onions
- 1 cup seeded and chopped green bell pepper
- 1 cup thinly sliced celery
- 2 cloves garlic, minced
- 1 1/2 teaspoons paprika
- 1/2 teaspoon freshly ground black pepper
- 1/4 teaspoon salt
- 1/4 teaspoon hot pepper sauce, such as Tabasco
- 1 bay leaf
- One 6-ounce can tomato paste
- 1 1/2 pounds raw medium-size shrimp (31 to 35 count), peeled and deveined
- 1 medium-size bunch green onions (white part and a few inches of the green), chopped
- 1 tablespoon filé powder

For Serving:
- 3 cups hot cooked white or pecan rice
- Hot pepper sauce, such as Tabasco

1. Combine the tomatoes with their juice, the broth, onions, bell pepper, celery, garlic, paprika, black pepper, salt, hot pepper sauce, and bay leaf in the slow cooker; stir in the tomato paste. Cover and cook on LOW for 5 to 6 hours or on HIGH for 2 1/2 to 3 hours.
2. Discard the bay leaf. Stir the shrimp, green onions, and filé powder into the hot tomato-vegetable mixture, cover, and cook until the shrimp are cooked through, about 5 minutes. Serve immediately over hot cooked rice with a bottle of hot pepper sauce on the side.

56 | *The XXL Slow Cooker Cookbook*

Shrimp Jambalaya

Prep time: 15 minutes | Cook time: 2¼ hours | Serves 8

- 2 tbsp. margarine
- 2 medium onions, chopped
- 2 green bell peppers, chopped
- 3 ribs celery, chopped
- 1 cup chopped, cooked lean ham
- 2 garlic cloves, chopped
- 1½ cups minute rice, uncooked
- 1½ cups fat-free low sodium beef broth
- 28-oz. can low-sodium chopped tomatoes
- 2 tbsp. chopped parsley, fresh **or** dried
- 1 tsp. dried basil
- ½ tsp. dried thyme
- ¼ tsp. black pepper
- ⅛ tsp. cayenne pepper
- 1 lb. shelled, deveined, medium-sized shrimp
- 1 tbsp. chopped parsley for garnish

1. One-half hour before assembling recipe, melt margarine in slow cooker set on High. Add onions, peppers, celery, ham, and garlic. Cook 30 minutes.
2. Add rice. Cover and cook 15 minutes.
3. Add broth, tomatoes, 2 tbsp. parsley, and remaining seasonings. Cover and cook on High 1 hour.
4. Add shrimp. Cook on High 30 minutes, or until liquid is absorbed.
5. Garnish with 1 tbsp. parsley.

Confetti Seafood Chowder

Prep time: 10 minutes | Cook time: 5 to 6 hour | Serves 4

- 1 1/2 tablespoons unsalted butter
- 1 small yellow onion, finely chopped
- 3 ribs celery, finely chopped
- 1 large or 2 small red bell peppers, seeded and finely chopped
- 2 medium-size russet potatoes, peeled and cut into 1/2-inch dice
- 2 cups chicken broth
- 1/2 bay leaf
- 1/8 teaspoon paprika
- 1 teaspoon dried thyme or 1 tablespoon chopped fresh thyme
- 1/4 teaspoon freshly ground black pepper
- 1/2 teaspoon salt or to taste
- 2 cups whole milk
- 1 cup half-and-half
- 2 cups frozen corn kernels, thawed
- 1 pound shellfish, white-fleshed fish fillets, or a combination (choose fresh or individually quick-frozen shellfish), cleaned or shelled and cut into chunks, if necessary

1. In a medium-size skillet, heat the butter over medium-high heat. Add the onion and celery and cook, stirring a few times, until the onion is transparent, 2 to 3 minutes. Add the bell pepper and cook until it begins to soften, 2 to 3 minutes longer.
2. While the vegetables are cooking, put the potatoes in the slow cooker.
3. When the vegetables are ready, scrape them into the cooker along with any remaining butter. Add the broth, bay leaf, paprika, thyme, and black pepper. If the broth is unsalted, add the 1/2 teaspoon salt. Stir the top layer of the ingredients very gently, trying not to disturb the potatoes, which should stay submerged. Cover and cook on LOW until the potatoes are fork-tender, 5 to 6 hours.
4. Add the milk, half-and-half, corn, and seafood and stir to combine. Cover and cook on HIGH until the chowder is heated through and the seafood is just cooked through, about 1 hour longer. Taste for salt and pepper. Remove the bay leaf before serving.

Chapter 7

Rice, Grains, and Beans

Kale & White Bean Chili

Prep time: 15 minutes, plus 8 hours to soak | Cook time: 6 to 8 hours on low | Serves 4 to 6

- 2 cups dried cannellini beans, soaked in water overnight, drained, and rinsed well
- 1 small bunch kale, washed, chopped, and de-ribbed
- 1 small onion, diced
- ½ green bell pepper, seeded and chopped
- 1 (4-ounce) can hatch green chiles
- 4 cups vegetable broth
- ½ teaspoon garlic powder
- 1 teaspoon chili powder
- ½ teaspoon ground cumin
- 2 tablespoons extra-virgin olive oil
- 1 avocado, peeled, pitted, and chopped

1. In your slow cooker, combine the beans, kale, onion, bell pepper, chiles, broth, garlic powder, chili powder, and cumin. Stir to mix the ingredients.
2. Cover the cooker and set to low. Cook for 6 to 8 hours.
3. Drizzle each bowl with olive oil, top with avocado, and serve.

Super Green Beans

Prep time: 15 minutes | Cook time: 1-2 hours | Serves 5

- 2 14½-oz. cans green beans, undrained
- 1 cup cooked cubed ham
- ⅓ cup finely chopped onion
- 1 tbsp. butter, melted, **or** bacon drippings

1. Place undrained beans in cooker. Add remaining ingredients and mix well.
2. Cook on High 1-2 hours, or until steaming hot.

Balsamic-Glazed Beets

Prep time: 15 minutes | Cook time: 2 hours | Serves 6

- 1 lb. beets, sliced
- 5 oz. orange juice
- 3 oz. balsamic vinegar
- 3 tbsp. almonds
- 6 oz. goat cheese
- 1 tsp. minced garlic
- 1 tsp. olive oil

1. Toss the beets with balsamic vinegar, orange juice, and olive oil in the insert of the slow cooker.
2. Put the slow cooker's lid on and set the cooking time to 7 hours on Low settings.
3. Toss goat cheese with minced garlic and almonds in a bowl.
4. Spread this cheese garlic mixture over the beets.
5. Put the cooker's lid on and set the cooking time to 10 minutes on High settings.
6. Serve warm.

The XXL Slow Cooker Cookbook | 59

Cheesy Slow Cooker Pizza

Prep time: 20 minutes | Cook time: 3-4 hours | Serves 6-8

- 1½ lbs. ground beef **or** bulk Italian sausage
- 1 medium onion, chopped
- 1 green pepper, chopped
- half a box rigatoni, cooked
- 7-oz. jar sliced mushrooms, drained
- 3 oz. sliced pepperoni
- 16-oz. jar pizza sauce
- 10 oz. mozzarella cheese, shredded
- 10 oz. cheddar cheese, shredded

1. Brown ground beef and onions in saucepan. Drain.
2. Layer half of each of the following, in the order given, in slow cooker: ground beef and onions, green pepper, noodles, mushrooms, pepperoni, pizza sauce, cheddar cheese, and mozzarella cheese. Repeat layers.
3. Cover. Cook on Low 3-4 hours.

Pasta Sauce with Meat and Veggies

Prep time: 10 minutes | Cook time: 7-8 hours | Serves 6

- ½ lb. ground turkey
- ½ lb. ground beef
- 1 rib celery, chopped
- 2 medium carrots, chopped
- 1 garlic clove, minced
- 1 medium onion, chopped
- 28-oz. can diced tomatoes with juice
- ½ tsp. salt
- ¼ tsp. dried thyme
- 6-oz. can tomato paste
- ⅛ tsp. pepper

1. Combine turkey, beef, celery, carrots, garlic, and onion in slow cooker.
2. Add remaining ingredients. Mix well.
3. Cover. Cook on Low 7-8 hours.
4. Serve over pasta or rice.

Green Chile and Sour Cream Rice Casserole

Prep time: 10 minutes | Cook time: 4 to 5 hours 30 minutes | Serves 6 to 8

- ½ cup (1 stick) unsalted butter
- 1 medium onion, finely chopped
- 1 Anaheim chile, seeded and finely chopped
- 1 medium red bell pepper, seeded and finely chopped
- 1 medium yellow or orange bell pepper, seeded and finely chopped
- 2 cups corn kernels, fresh off the cob or frozen and defrosted
- 1 teaspoon ground cumin
- ½ teaspoon ancho chile powder
- 1 cup milk
- 3 cups sour cream
- 4 cups cooked white rice
- 1½ cups finely shredded mild Cheddar cheese
- 1 cup finely shredded Monterey Jack cheese

1. Coat the insert of a 5- to 7-quart slow cooker with nonstick cooking spray or line it with a slow-cooker liner according to the manufacturer's directions.
2. Heat the butter in a large skillet over medium-high heat. Add the onion, chile, bell peppers, corn, cumin, and chile powder and sauté until the vegetables are softened, 5 to 7 minutes.
3. Remove from the heat and transfer the mixture to a large mixing bowl to cool. Once the vegetables are cool, stir in the milk and sour cream, rice, 1 cup of the Cheddar, and ½ cup of the Monterey Jack cheese and stir to combine.
4. Serve from the cooker set on warm.

Greek-Style Green Beans

Prep time: 5 minutes | Cook time: 2-5 hours | Serves 6

- 20 ozs. whole or cut-up frozen beans (not French cut)
- 2 cups tomato sauce
- 2 tsp. dried onion flakes, optional
- pinch of dried marjoram or oregano
- pinch of ground nutmeg
- pinch of cinnamon

1. Combine all ingredients in slow cooker, mixing together thoroughly.
2. Cover and cook on Low 2-4 hours if the beans are defrosted, or 3-5 hours on Low if the beans are frozen, or until the beans are done to your liking.

Slow-Cooked Wild Rice

Prep time: 15 minutes | Cook time: 4 hours | Makes 8 cups

- 1 lb. bulk pork sausage
- 4 celery ribs, chopped
- 1 small onion, chopped
- 1 can (10 $3/4$ oz.) condensed cream of mushroom soup, undiluted
- 1 can (10 $3/4$ oz.) condensed cream of chicken soup, undiluted
- 1 cup uncooked wild rice
- 1 can (4 oz.) mushroom stems and pieces, drained
- 3 cups chicken broth

1. In a large skillet, cook and crumble sausage with celery and onion over medium heat until sausage is no longer pink and vegetables are tender, 6-8 minutes; drain. Transfer to a 3-qt. slow cooker. Add soups, rice and mushrooms. Stir in broth.
2. Cook, covered, on low until rice is tender, 4-5 hours.

Herbed Harvest Rice

Prep time: 15 minutes, plus 8 hours to soak | Cook time: 3 hours on high | Serves 4 to 6

- 2 cups brown rice, soaked in water overnight, drained, and rinsed
- ½ small onion, chopped
- 4 cups vegetable broth
- 2 tablespoons extra-virgin olive oil
- ½ teaspoon dried thyme leaves
- ½ teaspoon garlic powder
- ½ cup cooked sliced mushrooms
- ½ cup dried cranberries
- ½ cup toasted pecans

1. In your slow cooker, combine the rice, onion, broth, olive oil, thyme, and garlic powder. Stir well.
2. Cover the cooker and set to high. Cook for 3 hours.
3. Stir in the mushrooms, cranberries, and pecans, and serve.

The XXL Slow Cooker Cookbook | 61

Special Green Beans

Prep time: 30-45 minutes | Cook time: 1-2 hours | Serves 12-14

- 4 14½-oz. cans green beans, drained
- 10¾-oz. can cream of mushroom soup
- 14½-oz. can chicken broth
- 1 cup tater tots
- 3-oz. can French-fried onion rings

1. Put green beans in slow cooker.
2. In a bowl, mix soup and broth together. Spread over beans.
3. Spoon tater tots over all. Top with onion rings.
4. Cover and bake on High 1-2 hours, or until heated through and potatoes are cooked.

Barbecued Baked Beans

Prep time: 10 minutes | Cook time: 3-4 hours | Serves 8-10

- 2 16-oz. cans baked beans, your choice of variety
- 2 15-oz. cans kidney **or** pinto beans, **or** one of each, drained
- ½ cup brown sugar
- 1 cup ketchup
- 1 onion, chopped

1. Combine all ingredients in slow cooker. Mix well.
2. Cover and cook on Low 3-4 hours, or until heated through.

Coconutty Brown Rice

Prep time: 15 minutes, plus 8 hours to soak | Cook time: 3 hours on high | Serves 4 to 6

- 2 cups brown rice, soaked in water overnight, drained, and rinsed
- 3 cups water
- 1½ cups full-fat coconut milk
- 1 teaspoon sea salt
- ½ teaspoon ground ginger
- freshly ground black pepper

1. In your slow cooker, combine the rice, water, coconut milk, salt, and ginger. Season with pepper and stir to incorporate the spices.
2. Cover the cooker and set to high. Cook for 3 hours and serve.

Cauliflower Rice and Spinach

Prep time: 15 minutes | Cook time: 3 hours | Serves 8

- 2 garlic cloves, minced
- 2 tbsp. butter, melted
- 1 yellow onion, chopped
- ¼ teaspoon thyme, dried
- 3 cups veggie stock
- 20 ounces spinach, chopped
- 6 ounces coconut cream
- salt and black pepper to the taste
- 2 cups cauliflower rice

1. Heat up a pan with the butter over medium heat, add onion, stir and cook for 4 minutes.
2. Add garlic, thyme, and stock, stir, cook for 1 minute more and transfer to your slow cooker.
3. Divide between plates and serve as a side dish.

Chicken and Triple Mushroom Casserole

Prep time: 10 minutes | Cook time: 2 to 3 hours 45 minutes | Serves 6 to 8

- ½ cup (1 stick) unsalted butter
- 1 medium onion, finely chopped
- 1½ pounds assorted mushrooms, such as button, cremini, shiitake, trumpet, and oyster, coarsely chopped
- 1 teaspoon dried thyme
- 1½ teaspoons salt
- ½ teaspoon freshly ground black pepper
- ¼ cup Marsala wine
- Grated zest of 1 lemon
- ½ cup finely chopped dried apricots (about 5)
- 3 cups cooked chicken, cut into bite-sized pieces or shredded
- 4 cups cooked wild rice
- 1½ cups chicken broth

1. Coat the insert of a 5- to 7-quart slow cooker with nonstick cooking spray or line it with a slow-cooker liner according to the manufacturer's directions.
2. Melt the butter in a large skillet over medium-high heat. Add the onion, mushrooms, thyme, salt, and pepper and sauté until the mushrooms begin to turn golden, 5 to 7 minutes. Stir in the Marsala, remove from the heat, and set aside to cool.
3. Put the remaining ingredients in the slow-cooker insert. Add the cooled mushrooms and stir to combine. Cover and cook on high for 2 to 3 hours, until the casserole is cooked through. Remove the cover and cook until the liquid is absorbed, an additional 30 to 45 minutes.
4. Serve from the cooker set on warm.

Easy Baked Beans

Prep time: 10 minutes | Cook time: 2 hours | Serves 8

- 2 16-oz. cans baked beans
- ¼ cup brown sugar
- ½ tsp. dried mustard
- ½ cup ketchup
- 2 small onions, chopped
- 1 tsp. Worcestershire sauce

1. Combine all ingredients in slow cooker.
2. Cover. Cook on High 2 hours.

Slimmed-Down Spaghetti Sauce

Prep time: 15 minutes | Cook time: 6-8 hours | Serves 8

- 2 tsp. olive oil
- 1 medium onion, finely chopped
- 6 cloves garlic, minced
- 56-oz. can low-sodium crushed tomatoes, **or** 7 cups fresh, peeled, diced tomatoes
- 6-oz. can low-sodium tomato paste
- 2 tsp. dried basil
- ½ tsp. dried oregano
- 1 tsp. salt
- ½ tsp. black pepper
- 1 tbsp. sugar
- 2 tbsp. chopped fresh parsley

1. Heat oil in a saucepan over medium heat. Add onion and garlic. Sauté until onion becomes very soft (about 10 minutes).
2. Combine all ingredients except parsley in slow cooker.
3. Cover. Cook on Low 6-8 hours.
4. Add parsley. Cook an additional 30 minutes.
5. Serve over cooked noodles.

Barbecued Green Beans

Prep time: 20 minutes | Cook time: 3-8 hours | Serves 4-6

- 1 lb. bacon
- ¼ cup chopped onions
- ¾ cup ketchup
- ½ cup brown sugar
- 3 tsp. Worcestershire sauce
- ¾ tsp. salt
- 4 cups green beans

1. Brown bacon in skillet until crisp and then break into pieces. Reserve 2 tbsp. bacon drippings.
2. Sauté onions in bacon drippings.
3. Combine ketchup, brown sugar, Worcestershire sauce, and salt. Stir into bacon and onions.
4. Pour mixture over green beans and mix lightly.
5. Pour into slow cooker and cook on High 3-4 hours, or on Low 6-8 hours.

Herby Slow Cooker Pizza

Prep time: 20 minutes | Cook time: 1-2½ hours | Serves 8

- 1 lb. extra-lean ground beef
- 2 small onions, chopped
- 14-oz. can fat-free pizza sauce
- 14-oz. can low-fat, low-sodium spaghetti sauce
- 1 tsp. garlic powder
- 1¼ tsp. black pepper
- 1 tsp. dried oregano
- ¼ tsp. rubbed sage
- 12 ozs. dry kluski noodles

1. Brown ground beef and onions in nonstick skillet.
2. In skillet, or in a large bowl, mix together browned meat and onions, pizza sauce, spaghetti sauce, and seasonings and herbs.
3. Boil noodles according to directions on package until tender. Drain.
4. Layer half of beef sauce in bottom of cooker. Spoon in noodles. Top with remaining beef sauce.
5. Cook on Low 1-1½ hours if ingredients are hot when placed in cooker. If the sauce and noodles are at room temperature or have just been refrigerated, cook on High for 2-2½ hours.

Fiesta Corn and Beans

Prep time: 25 minutes | Cook time: 3 hours | Serves 10

- 1 large onion, chopped
- 1 medium green pepper, cut into 1-inch pieces
- 1 to 2 jalapeno peppers, seeded and sliced
- 1 tablespoon olive oil
- 1 garlic clove, minced
- 2 cans (16 ounces each) kidney beans, rinsed and drained
- 1 package (16 ounces) frozen corn
- 1 can (14 ½ ounces) diced tomatoes, undrained
- 1 teaspoon chili powder
- ¾ teaspoon salt
- ½ teaspoon ground cumin
- ½ teaspoon pepper

Optional Toppings:
- plain yogurt and sliced ripe olives

1. In a large skillet, saute onion and peppers in oil until tender. Add garlic; cook 1 minute longer. Transfer to a 4-qt. slow cooker. Stir in the beans, corn, tomatoes and seasonings.
2. Cover and cook on low for 3-4 hours or until heated through. Serve with yogurt and olives if desired.

Chapter 8

Vegan and Vegetarian

Zuppa Toscana

Prep time: 15 minutes or fewer | Cook time: 5 to 6 hours on low | Serves 4 to 6

- 4 cups vegetable broth
- 2 cups chopped de-ribbed kale
- 2 small sweet potatoes, peeled and diced
- 1 medium zucchini, diced
- 1 (15-ounce) can cannellini beans, rinsed and drained well
- 1 carrot, diced
- 1 small onion, diced
- ½ teaspoon garlic powder
- ½ teaspoon sea salt
- ¼ teaspoon red pepper flakes
- freshly ground black pepper

1. In your slow cooker, combine the broth, kale, sweet potatoes, zucchini, beans, celery, carrot, onion, garlic powder, salt, and red pepper flakes, and season with black pepper.
2. Cover the cooker and set to low. Cook for 5 to 6 hours and serve.

Green Pea Casserole

Prep time: 15 minutes | Cook time: 20 minutes | Serves 8

- 5 cups frozen peas (about 20 oz.), thawed
- 1 celery rib, chopped
- ½ cup mayonnaise
- ⅓ cup chopped onion
- ¼ tsp. salt
- ¼ tsp. pepper
- 1 pkg. (6 oz.) stuffing mix

1. Preheat oven to 350°. Mix first six ingredients; transfer to a greased 11x7-in baking dish. Prepare stuffing mix according to package directions.
2. Spread over pea mixture. Bake casserole, uncovered, until lightly browned, 20-25 minutes.

Cheesy Beer Dip Salsa

Prep time: 5 minutes | Cook time: 4 hours | Serves 5 ½ cups

- 16 oz salsa
- 2/3 cup beer
- 1 lb. American cheese, shredded
- 8 oz cream cheese, sliced
- 8 oz Monterey jack cheese, shredded

1. Begin by combining all the ingredients until they are properly mixed.
2. Cover the slow cooker and cook for 4 hours on low heat.
3. Serve immediately.

Creamy Mashed Potatoes

Prep time: 10-15 minutes | Cook time: 3-5 hours | Serves 10-12

- 2 tsp. salt
- 6 tbsp. (¾ stick) butter, melted
- 2¼ cups milk
- 6 ⅞ cups potato flakes
- 1 cup sour cream
- 4-5 ozs. (approximately half of a large pkg.) cream cheese, softened

1. Combine first five ingredients as directed on potato box.
2. Whip cream cheese with electric mixer until creamy. Blend in sour cream.
3. Fold potatoes into cheese and sour cream. Beat well. Place in slow cooker.
4. Cover. Cook on Low 3-5 hours.

Creamy Carrot Casserole

Prep time: 15 minutes | Cook time: 30 minutes | Serves 8

- 1 1/2 lbs. carrots, sliced or 1 pkg. (20 oz.) frozen sliced carrots, thawed
- 1 cup mayonnaise
- 1 tbsp. grated onion
- 1 tbsp. prepared horseradish
- 1/4 cup shredded cheddar cheese
- 2 tbsp. crushed Ritz crackers

1. Preheat oven to 350°. Place 1 in. of water in a large saucepan; add carrots. Bring to a boil. Reduce heat; cover and simmer until crisp-tender, 7-9 minutes. Drain, reserving 1/4 cup cooking liquid. Transfer carrots to a 1 1/2-qt. baking dish.
2. In a small bowl, combine the mayonnaise, onion, horseradish and reserved cooking liquid; spread evenly over carrots. Sprinkle with cheese; top with cracker crumbs. Bake, uncovered, for 30 minutes.

Elbows Casserole

Prep time: 5 minutes | Cook time: 5 1/2 hours | Serves 4

- 1 packet low | Carb: elbows or ravioli, cooked
- 1/4 cup Romano cheese, preferably grated
- 1/4 cup black olives, sliced
- 2 cup low | Carb: BBQ sauce
- 2 cup mushrooms, preferably sliced
- 1 cup of small curd cottage cheese

1. Coat your slow cooker with oil.
2. Spoon the BBQ sauce into it and then top with 1/2 of the cooked elbows, half of the Romano cheese and mushrooms along with 2 tbsp of the olives.
3. Continue layering with the remaining ingredients.
4. Cook within 5 1/2 hours on low heat or until cooked.
5. Sprinkle with the cottage cheese and cook again for another half an hour.

Asian-Style Broccoli

Prep time: 15 minutes | Cook time: 6 hours | Serves 8

- 2 lbs. fresh broccoli, trimmed and chopped into bite-size pieces
- 1 clove garlic, minced
- 1 green or red bell pepper, cut into thin slices
- 1 onion, cut into slices
- 4 tbsp. light soy sauce
- 1/2 tsp. salt
- dash of black pepper
- 1 tbsp. sesame seeds as garnish, optional

1. Combine all ingredients except sesame seeds in slow cooker.
2. Cook on Low for 6 hours. Top with sesame seeds.
3. Serve on brown rice.

Golden Cauliflower

Prep time: 5-10 minutes | Cook time: 1½-5 hours | Serves 4-6

- 2 10-oz. pkgs. frozen cauliflower, thawed
- salt and pepper
- 10¾-oz. can condensed cheddar cheese soup
- 4 slices bacon, crisply fried and crumbled

1. Place cauliflower in slow cooker. Season with salt and pepper.
2. Spoon soup over top. Sprinkle with bacon.
3. Cover and cook on High 1½ hours, or on Low 4-5 hours, or until cauliflower is tender.

Indian-Spiced Cauliflower

Prep time: 15 minutes or fewer | Cook time: 3 to 4 hours on low | Serves 4 to 6

- 1 large head cauliflower, leaves and large stem removed
- ½ medium onion, diced
- 2 tablespoons extra-virgin olive oil
- ½ teaspoon sea salt
- ½ teaspoon garlic powder
- ½ teaspoon ground ginger
- ½ teaspoon curry powder
- ¼ teaspoon ground turmeric
- ¼ teaspoon ground cumin
- ⅛ teaspoon cayenne pepper

1. Chop the cauliflower into florets, and place them in the slow cooker with the onion.
2. In a small bowl, combine the olive oil, salt, garlic powder, ginger, curry powder, turmeric, cumin, and cayenne. Whisk into a paste. Using a pastry brush or a spoon, spread the spice paste onto the cauliflower florets.
3. Cover the cooker and set to low. Cook for 3 to 4 hours and serve.

Apricot-Glazed Carrots

Prep time: 5 minutes | Cook time: 9¼ hours | Serves 8

- 2 lbs. baby carrots
- 1 onion, chopped
- ½ cup water
- ⅓ cup honey
- ⅓ cup apricot preserves
- 2 tbsp. chopped fresh parsley

1. Place carrots and onions in slow cooker. Add water.
2. Cover and cook on Low 9 hours.
3. Drain liquid from slow cooker.
4. In a small bowl, mix honey and preserves together. Pour over carrots.
5. Cover and cook on High 10-15 minutes.
6. Sprinkle with parsley before serving.

Braised Cabbage

Prep time: 5 minutes | Cook time: 5 hours | Serves 2

- 1 green cabbage head, tough ends discarded and cut into 12 wedges
- ½ cup bone broth
- 1 sweet onion, preferably large and chopped
- ¼ cup bacon fat, melted
- 4 garlic cloves
- Celtic sea salt, preferably coarse
- caraway seeds

1. Heat the slow cooker on high heat and then add melted bacon | Fat: and onions to it.
2. After that, place the cabbage wedges in a layer in the slow cooker.
3. Spoon the broth over it along with the salt and caraway seeds.
4. Cover the slow cooker, then cook within 1 hour.
5. In between, stir the cabbage once to shift the top ones to the bottom.
6. Pour in more stock if required.
7. Cook it again for another 4 hours on high heat.
8. Once cooked, you can add some apple cider vinegar if you like.

Maple-Dijon Brussels Sprouts

Prep time: 15 minutes or fewer | Cook time: 3 to 4 hours on low | Serves 4 to 6

- 1 pound brussels sprouts, ends trimmed
- 2 tablespoons maple syrup
- 1 tablespoon dijon mustard
- ½ teaspoon garlic powder
- ½ teaspoon sea salt
- ¼ cup water

1. In your slow cooker, combine the Brussels sprouts, maple syrup, mustard, garlic powder, salt, and water. Toss together to distribute evenly.
2. Cover the cooker and set to low. Cook for 3 to 4 hours and serve.

Golden Carrots

Prep time: 5 minutes | Cook time: 3-4 hours | Serves 6

- 2-lb. pkg. baby carrots
- ½ cup golden raisins
- 1 stick (½ cup) butter, melted or softened
- ⅓ cup honey
- 2 tbsp. lemon juice
- ½ tsp. ground ginger, optional

1. Combine all ingredients in slow cooker.
2. Cover and cook on Low 3-4 hours, or until carrots are tender-crisp.

Brussels Sprout Dip

Prep time: 10 minutes | Cook time: 1 to 2 hours | Serves 4

- 1 lb. Brussels sprouts, quartered
- ¼ cup parmesan cheese, grated
- 1 garlic clove, unpeeled
- ¼ cup sour cream
- 1 tbsp olive oil
- ½ tsp thyme, chopped
- ¾ cup mozzarella, shredded
- 4 oz cream cheese, room temperature
- ¼ cup mayonnaise

1. Combine Brussels sprouts with pepper, olive oil, and salt and then spread them in a baking sheet in a single layer along with garlic Roast in a preheated oven at 400 degrees F for about 25 to 30 minutes while flipping them repeatedly.
2. Place all the other remaining ingredients into the slow cooker and stir well.
3. Stir in the Brussels sprouts.
4. Cook within 1 to 2 hours on high heat or until the cheese has melted.

Garlic Mashed Potatoes

Prep time: 20 minutes | Cook time: 4-7 hours | Serves 6

- 2 lbs. baking potatoes, unpeeled and cut into ½-inch cubes
- ¼ cup water
- 3 tbsp. butter, sliced
- 1 tsp. salt
- ¾ tsp. garlic powder
- ¼ tsp. black pepper
- 1 cup milk

1. Combine all ingredients, except milk, in slow cooker. Toss to combine.
2. Cover. Cook on Low 7 hours, or on High 4 hours.
3. Add milk to potatoes during last 30 minutes of cooking time.
4. Mash potatoes with potato masher or electric mixer until fairly smooth.
5. Serve immediately, or if making ahead, allow to cool and chill in fridge.
6. Place in slow cooker 2 hours before serving. Cover. Set cooker on Low.
7. Stir before serving.

Balsamic Beets

Prep time: 15 minutes or fewer | Cook time: 4 to 6 hours on low | Serves 4 to 6

- 4 to 6 medium beets (they need to fit snugly in the bottom of your slow cooker), chopped (see tip)
- ½ cup balsamic vinegar
- 1 cup apple juice
- ½ teaspoon garlic powder
- ½ teaspoon dried rosemary
- freshly ground black pepper

1. In your slow cooker, combine the beets, vinegar, apple juice, garlic powder, and rosemary, and season with pepper.
2. Cover the cooker and set to low. Cook for 6 to 8 hours and serve.

Broccoli Delight

Prep time: 15 minutes | Cook time: 2-6 hours | Serves 4-6

- 1-2 lbs. broccoli, chopped
- 2 cups cauliflower, chopped
- 10¾-oz. can 98% fat-free cream of celery soup
- ½ tsp. salt
- ¼ tsp. black pepper
- 1 medium onion, diced
- 2-4 garlic cloves, crushed, according to your taste preference
- ½ cup vegetable broth

1. Combine all ingredients in slow cooker.
2. Cook on Low 4-6 hours, or on High 2-3 hours.

Lentil Bolognese

Prep time: 15 minutes, plus 8 hours to soak | Cook time: 30 minutes on high plus 5 to 6 hours on low | Serves 4 to 6

- 1 tablespoon extra-virgin olive oil
- 2 carrots, grated
- 1 celery stalk, minced
- 1 small onion, diced
- ½ teaspoon garlic powder
- 4 cups diced tomatoes
- 2 cups vegetable broth
- 1 cup lentils, soaked in water overnight, drained, and rinsed well
- 1 bay leaf
- ½ teaspoon dried oregano
- ½ teaspoon dried basil leaves
- ½ teaspoon sea salt
- ¼ teaspoon red pepper flakes
- ¼ teaspoon ground nutmeg
- freshly ground black pepper

1. Coat the slow cooker with the olive oil. Add the carrots, celery, onion, and garlic powder.
2. Cover the cooker and set to high. Cook for 30 minutes.
3. Stir in the tomatoes, broth, lentils, bay leaf, oregano, basil, salt, red pepper flakes, and nutmeg, then season with black pepper. Re-cover the cooker and set to low. Cook for 5 to 6 hours.
4. Remove and discard the bay leaf before serving.

Chapter 9

Soups, Stews and Chilis

Anything Goes Sausage Soup

Prep time: 40 minutes | Cook time: 9 ½ hours | Serves 15

- 1 pound bulk pork sausage
- 4 cups water
- 1 can (10 ¾ ounces) condensed cream of mushroom soup, undiluted
- 1 can (10 ¾ ounces) condensed cheddar cheese soup, undiluted
- 5 medium red potatoes, cubed
- 4 cups chopped cabbage
- 3 large carrots, thinly sliced
- 4 celery ribs, chopped
- 1 medium zucchini, chopped
- 1 large onion, chopped
- 5 chicken bouillon cubes
- 1 tablespoon dried parsley flakes
- ¾ teaspoon pepper
- 1 can (12 ounces) evaporated milk

1. In a large skillet, cook sausage over medium heat until no longer pink, breaking it up into crumbles; drain. Transfer to a 6-qt. slow cooker. Stir in water and soups until blended. Add the vegetables, chicken bouillon, parsley and pepper.
2. Cover; cook on low for 9-10 hours or until the vegetables are tender. Stir in the evaporated milk; cover and cook 30 minutes longer.

Wintertime Meatball Soup

Prep time: 20 minutes | Cook time: 9 hours | Serves 15

- 2 cans (16 ounces each) chili beans, undrained
- 2 cans (14 ½ ounces each) beef broth
- 1 jar (26 ounces) spaghetti sauce
- ¼ cup chopped onion
- 3 garlic cloves, minced
- 1 tablespoon Worcestershire sauce
- 1 teaspoon Italian seasoning
- 1 package (32 ounces) frozen fully cooked Italian meatballs
- 1 package (16 ounces) frozen mixed vegetables
- 4 cups chopped cabbage

1. In a 6-qt. slow cooker, combine the chili beans, beef broth, spaghetti sauce, onion, garlic, Worcestershire sauce and Italian seasoning.
2. Stir in Italian meatballs, mixed vegetables and cabbage. Cover and cook on low for 8-10 hours or until the vegetables are tender.

Ginger Pear Pumpkin Soup

Prep time: 10 minutes | Cook time: 3 hours 30 minutes | Serves 8

- 4 tablespoons (½ stick) unsalted butter
- ½ cup finely chopped sweet onion
- ½ cup finely chopped celery
- ½ cup finely chopped carrot
- 2 medium red pears, peeled, cored, and finely chopped
- ½ teaspoon ground ginger
- 3 cups chicken broth
- Salt and freshly ground black pepper
- 1 cup heavy cream

1. Melt the butter in a medium skillet over medium-high heat. Add the onion, celery, carrot, pears, and ginger and sauté until the vegetables begin to soften, about 3 minutes. Transfer the contents of the skillet to the insert of a 5- to 7-quart slow cooker.
2. Stir in the pumpkin and broth. Cover and cook on high for 3 hours or on low for 5 to 6 hours.
3. Season with salt and pepper. Stir in the cream, cover, and leave on warm for 30 minutes before serving.

Roasted Tomato Soup with Spinach Pesto

Prep time: 10 minutes | Cook time: 6 hours | Serves 8

Soup
- Two 28-ounce cans peeled whole tomatoes, drained
- ½ cup extra-virgin olive oil
- 2 teaspoons dried basil
- 1 teaspoon dried marjoram
- ½ cup chopped red onion
- 6 cloves garlic, coarsely chopped
- 1½ teaspoons salt
- Pinch red pepper flakes
- ½ cup vegetable or chicken broth
- 1 cup whole-milk ricotta cheese
- 1½ cups heavy cream
- ½ cup freshly grated Parmigiano-Reggiano
- Spinach Pesto (recipe follows)

Spinach Pesto
- Two 10-ounce packages baby spinach
- ½ cup pine nuts
- 2 cloves garlic, peeled
- Grated zest of 1 lemon
- ½ cup packed fresh basil leaves
- ½ cup freshly grated Parmesan cheese
- 2/3 cup olive oil
- Salt and freshly ground black pepper

1. Combine the tomatoes, olive oil, basil, marjoram, onion, garlic, salt, pepper flakes, and broth in the insert of a 5- to 7-quart slow cooker.
2. Cover the slow cooker and cook on low for 6 hours, until the tomatoes and onion are softened. Using an immersion blender, purée the soup, or cool the soup and purée it in a blender or food processor. Whisk in the ricotta, cream, and Parmigiano-Reggiano.
3. Cover the cooker and turn it to warm. Allow the soup to come to serving temperature (the retained heat in the cooker will heat the cheese and cream, without it separating).
4. Serve the soup garnished with the spinach pesto.
5. Spinach pesto retains its bright green color and adds zip and color to roasted tomato soup, but it can also be tossed with pasta or as a sauce for pasta or potato salad.
6. Put the spinach, pine nuts, garlic, lemon zest, basil, and Parmesan cheese in the work bowl of a food processor or a blender. Pulse the food processor on and off until the leaves are chopped and the mixture is chunky. with the machine running, slowly pour in the oil and process until the mixture comes together.
7. Season with salt and pepper. Store the pesto, covered, in the refrigerator for up to 1 week or in the freezer for up to 6 weeks.

Delicious Chicken Soup with Lemongrass

Prep time: 5 minutes | Cook time: 8–10 hours | Serves 2

1 stalk lemongrass, cut into big hunks
1 whole chicken
1 tbsp. salt
5 thick slices of fresh ginger
20 fresh basil leaves, chopped
1 lime, juiced, or to taste

1. Place the lemongrass, ginger, half of the basil leaves, salt, and chicken into the slow cooker.
2. Fill the slow cooker up with water. Boil the chicken mixture for 8–10 hours.
3. Scoop the soup into a bowl and adjust the salt to taste. Add the lime juice to taste and spice up with the remaining chopped basil leaves.

Bone Broth

Prep time: 15 minutes | Cook time: 6–10 hours | Serves 2

- 3 ½ lb. mixed assorted bones
- 1 tbsp. pink Himalayan salt
- 1 parsnip
- 1 white onion, skin-on
- 5 garlic cloves, peeled
- 2 celery stalks
- 2 carrots
- 2 tbsp. cider vinegar or lemon juice
- 8 cups water
- ¼ cup Bay leaves

1. Peel and slice the vegetables, with the roots, into ⅓-inch pieces. Slice the onion in half. Chop the celery into thirds. Add the bay leaves into the slow cooker.
2. Toss in the chosen bones (can also be pork). Pour the water up to ¾ of the slow cooker's capacity along with the juice/vinegar and bay leaves. Sprinkle with salt.
3. Secure the slow cooker's lid. Cook on low for 10 hours or on High for 6 hours. (You can simmer for up to 48 hours.)
4. Use a strainer to remove the bits of veggies. Set the bones aside to chill. Then shred the meat.
5. Refrigerate the broth overnight. Scrape away the tallow (greasy layer) if desired. Use within 5 days or freeze it. You can also keep it in the canning jars for up to 45 days.

Creamy Loaded Baked-Potato Soup

Prep time: 10 minutes | Cook time: 5 to 6 hours | Serves 8 to 10

- 4 tablespoons (½ stick) unsalted butter
- 2 medium leeks, finely chopped, using the white and some of the tender green parts
- 4 large russet potatoes, peeled and cut into ½-inch dice (see savvy)
- 4 cups chicken broth
- 1 cup whole milk
- 2 cups finely shredded sharp Cheddar cheese
- 6 green onions, finely chopped, using the white and some of the tender green parts
- 8 strips bacon, cooked crisp, drained, and crumbled
- Salt and freshly ground black pepper
- 1 cup sour cream for garnishing

1. Heat the butter in a large skillet over medium-high heat. Add the leeks and sauté until softened, 2 to 3 minutes. Transfer the leeks to the insert of a 5- to 7-quart slow cooker and add the potatoes and broth. Cover the slow cooker and cook on high for 3 hours or on low for 5 to 6 hours, until the potatoes are tender. Using an immersion blender, purée the soup, or cool the soup and purée it in a blender.
2. Reduce the heat to low and add the milk, cheese, green onions, and bacon. Cover the slow cooker and cook for an additional 1 hour. Season with salt and pepper.
3. Serve the soup garnished with a dollop of sour cream.

Lotsa-Tomatoes Beef Stew

Prep time: 15 minutes | Cook time: 5½-6 hours | Serves 6

- 2 lbs. extra-lean stewing beef cubes, trimmed of fat
- 5-6 carrots, cut in 1-inch pieces
- 1 large onion, cut in chunks
- 3 ribs celery, sliced
- 6 medium tomatoes, cut up and gently mashed
- ½ cup quick-cooking tapioca
- 1 whole clove, **or** ¼-½ tsp. ground cloves
- 1 tsp. dried basil
- ½ tsp. dried oregano
- 2 bay leaves
- 2 tsp. salt
- ½ tsp. black pepper
- 3-4 potatoes, cubed

1. Place all ingredients in slow cooker. Mix together well.
2. Cover. Cook on High 5½-6 hours.

Italian Chicken Stew

Prep time: 20 minutes | Cook time: 3-6 hours | Serves 4

- 2 boneless, skinless chicken breast halves, uncooked, cut in 1½-inch pieces
- 19-oz. can cannellini beans, drained and rinsed
- 15½-oz. can kidney beans, drained and rinsed
- 14½-oz. can low-sodium diced tomatoes, undrained
- 1 cup chopped celery
- 1 cup sliced carrots
- 2 small garlic cloves, coarsely chopped
- 1 cup water
- ½ cup dry red wine **or** low-fat chicken broth
- 3 tbsp. tomato paste
- 1 tbsp. sugar
- 1½ tsp. dried Italian seasoning

1. Combine chicken, cannellini beans, kidney beans, tomatoes, celery, carrots, and garlic in slow cooker. Mix well.
2. In medium bowl, combine all remaining ingredients. Mix well. Pour over chicken and vegetables. Mix well.
3. Cover. Cook on Low 5-6 hours, or on High 3 hours.

Beef Barley Vegetable Soup

Prep time: 15 minutes | Cook time: 8 hours and 20 minutes | Serves 2

- 1 package frozen mixed vegetables
- Ground black pepper, to taste
- 1 beef chuck roast
- 1 onion, chopped
- salt, to taste
- ½ cup barley
- 4 cups water
- 1 can chop stewed tomatoes
- 1 bay leaf
- 3 stalks celery, chopped
- ¼ tsp. ground black pepper
- 3 carrots, chopped
- 4 pcs. beef bouillon cubes
- 2 tbsp. oil

1. Season your beef with salt, adding the bay leaf and the barley at the end. Cook the beef in the slow cooker for 8 hours, or until tender.
2. Set the beef aside; keep the broth also aside.
3. Stir-fry your onion, celery, carrots, and frozen vegetable. Mix until soft.
4. Add the bouillon cubes, pepper, water, salt, beef mixture, barley mixture, tomatoes, and broth.
5. Bring to a boiling point and simmer at lowered heat for 20 minutes.

Pumpkin Turkey Chili

Prep time: 15 minutes | Cook time: 6–8 hours | Serves 2

- 1 medium green bell pepper, diced
- 2 lb. ground turkey
- 6–8 garlic cloves
- 1 ½ cups chicken broth
- 1 (6-oz.) tomato paste
- 1 (15-oz.) pumpkin purée
- 1 (14 ½-oz.) diced tomatoes
- 1 ½ tsp. cinnamon
- 2 tbsp. chili powder
- 1 tsp. sea salt
- 1 tsp. ground cumin
- a pinch of ground pepper
- ½ tsp. onion powder

1. Place a skillet over the medium-High setting. Cook the garlic and peppers. Toss in the ground turkey and continue cooking until it is no longer pink. Break it up and add it to the slow cooker.
2. Add the rest of the ingredients to the slow cooker. Cook on low for 6–8 hours.

Chipotle Chicken Chili

Prep time: 20 minutes | Cook time: 7–8 hours | Serves 2

- 3 tbsp. extra-virgin olive oil, divided
- 1 lb. ground chicken
- ½ sweet onion, chopped
- 2 tsp. garlic, minced
- 1 (28-oz.) can diced tomatoes
- 1 cup chicken broth
- 1 cup pumpkin, diced
- 1 green bell pepper, diced
- 3 tbsp. chili powder
- 1 tsp. chipotle chili powder
- 1 cup sour cream, for garnishing
- 1 cup cheddar cheese, shredded, for garnishing

1. Lightly, grease the insert of the slow cooker with 1 tbsp. of olive oil.
2. In a large skillet over medium-High heat, heat the remaining olive oil. Add the chicken and sauté until it is cooked for about 6 minutes.
3. Add the onion and garlic and sauté for an additional 3 minutes.
4. Transfer the chicken mixture to the insert and stir in the tomatoes, broth, pumpkin, bell pepper, chili powder, and chipotle chili powder.
5. Cover the slow cooker with the lid and cook on low for 7–8 hours.
6. Serve topped with sour cream and cheese.

White Chicken Chili

Prep time: 10 minutes | Cook time: 8 to 10 hours | Serves 8

- 3 tablespoons olive oil
- 2 medium onions, finely chopped
- 1 medium red bell pepper, seeded and finely chopped
- 1 medium green bell pepper, seeded and finely chopped
- 4 chipotle chiles in adobo, finely chopped (see savvy)
- 1 teaspoon ground cumin
- 1 teaspoon dried oregano
- 8 cups chicken broth
- Four 6-inch corn tortillas, torn into small pieces
- Two 14- to 15-ounce cans small white beans, drained and rinsed
- 3 cups cooked chicken or turkey
- One 16-ounce package frozen corn, defrosted
- ½ cup finely chopped fresh cilantro
- 2 cups finely shredded mild Cheddar or Monterey Jack cheese for garnishing
- 2 cups sour cream for garnishing

1. Heat the oil in a large skillet over medium-high heat. Add the onions, bell peppers, chiles, cumin, and oregano and sauté until the vegetables are softened, 5 to 7 minutes.
2. Transfer the contents of the skillet to the insert of a 5- to 7-quart slow cooker. Add the broth, tortillas, beans, chicken, and corn.
3. Cover the slow cooker and cook on low for 8 to 10 hours, until the chili is thick and the beans and vegetables are tender. Stir in the cilantro.
4. Serve each bowl garnished with cheese and sour cream.

Fennel Flavored Fish Stew

Prep time: 15 minutes | Cook time: 6 hours | Serves 4

- 1 lb. firm fish fillets, chopped
- ½ qt clam juice
- ¼ cup dry white wine
- 2 peeled and chopped medium tomatoes
- ½ cup carrots, chopped
- ½ cup onion, chopped
- 1 minced garlic cloves
- ½ tbsp minced orange zest
- ½ tsp lightly crushed fennel seeds
- 1/8 cup parsley chopped

1. In a slow cooker, mix all the ingredients, except the fish fillets, parsley, salt, and pepper.
2. Cook on low for 6 hours.
3. Add the fish within the last 15 minutes.
4. Add the parsley and stir to distribute—season with salt and pepper before serving.

The XXL Slow Cooker Cookbook | 77

Julia's Potato and Leek Soup

Prep time: 10 minutes | Cook time: 5 to 6 hours | Serves 8 to 10

- 4 tablespoons (½ stick) unsalted butter
- 4 leeks, finely chopped, using the white and a bit of the tender green parts
- 4 large russet potatoes, peeled and cut into 1-inch chunks
- 3 cups chicken broth
- Salt and freshly ground black pepper
- 1 cup heavy cream
- ½ cup snipped fresh chives for garnishing

1. Turn a 5- to 7-quart slow cooker on high, add the butter to the insert, and cover until the butter is melted. Add the leeks and toss with the butter. Add the potatoes and broth. Cover the slow cooker and cook the soup on high for 3 hours or on low for 5 to 6 hours, until the potatoes are tender.
2. Puree the soup with an immersion blender, or mash with a potato masher. Season with salt and pepper. Stir in the cream and turn off the slow cooker. Cool the soup, then refrigerate until chilled.
3. Serve the soup in chilled bowls and garnish with the chives.

White Chili

Prep time: 30 minutes | Cook time: 3 hours | Serves 12

- 3 cans (15 1/2 ounces each) great northern beans, rinsed and drained
- 3 cups cubed cooked chicken breast
- 1 jar (15 ounces) Alfredo sauce
- 2 cups chicken broth
- 1 to 2 cans (4 ounces each) chopped green chilies
- 1 ½ cups frozen gold and white corn
- 1 cup (4 ounces) shredded Monterey Jack cheese
- 1 cup (4 ounces) shredded pepper jack cheese
- 1 cup sour cream
- 1 small sweet yellow pepper, chopped
- 1 small onion, chopped
- 3 garlic cloves, minced
- 1 tablespoon ground cumin
- 1 ½ teaspoons white pepper
- 1 to 1 ½ teaspoons cayenne pepper
- salsa verde and chopped fresh cilantro, optional

1. In a 5- or 6-qt. slow cooker, combine the first 1Cover and cook on low for 3-4 hours or until heated though, stirring once. Serve with salsa verde and cilantro if desired.

Simple Texas Chili

Prep time: 19 minutes | Cook time: 7–8 hours | Serves 2

- ¼ cup extra-virgin olive oil
- 1 ½ lb. beef sirloin, cut into 1-inch chunks
- 1 sweet onion, chopped
- ½ tsp. ground cumin
- ¼ tsp. ground coriander
- 1 cup sour cream, for garnishing
- 1 avocado, diced, for garnishing
- 1 tbsp. cilantro, chopped, for garnishing

1. Lightly, grease the insert of the slow cooker with 1 tbsp. of olive oil.
2. In a large skillet over medium-High heat, heat the remaining olive oil. Add the beef and sauté until it is cooked for about 8 minutes.
3. Transfer the beef mixture to the insert and stir in the tomatoes, broth, chili powder, cumin, and coriander.
4. Cover and cook on low for 7–8 hours.
5. Serve topped with sour cream, avocado, and cilantro.

Creamy Broccoli Soup

Prep time: 10 minutes | Cook time: 5 to 6 hours | Serves 6 to 8

- 2 tablespoons unsalted butter
- 1 medium onion, finely chopped
- 3 medium carrots, cut into ½-inch dice
- 2 bunches broccoli (about 1½ pounds), stems trimmed, cut into florets
- 1 teaspoon baking soda
- 3 cups chicken or vegetable broth
- Salt and freshly ground black pepper
- 1 cup heavy cream (to lower the fat, use whole milk, or add more broth)

1. Turn a 5- to 7-quart slow cooker on high, add the butter to the insert, and cover until the butter is melted. Add the onion, carrots, and broccoli and toss the vegetables in the butter. Dissolve the baking soda in the broth and add to the vegetables.
2. Cook on high for 2½ to 3 hours or on low for 5 to 6 hours.
3. Season with salt and pepper and stir in the cream. Turn off the slow cooker and let the soup rest for 15 minutes to come to serving temperature.

Slow Cooker Pork Stew with Tapioca

Prep time: 15 minutes | Cook time: 9–10 hours | Serves 2

- 3 tbsp. quick-cooking tapioca
- ½ cup Vegetable oil
- ¼ tsp. pepper
- 1 large onion, chopped
- 1 ½ lb. pork stew meat, cut into bite-size pieces
- 1 tsp. Worcestershire sauce
- 1 celery stalk, chopped
- 2 pcs. Carrots, sliced
- 1 tbsp. beef bouillon granules
- 3 cups vegetable juice

1. Heat the oil in a Dutch oven over medium-High heat; brown your beef on all sides.
2. In the Slow cooker, mix the browned beef with all the other ingredients.
3. Cover and cook on low for 9–10 hours.

Golden Lentil Soup

Prep time: 15 minutes, plus 8 hours to soak | Cook time: 6 to 8 hours on low | Serves 4 to 6

- 1 cup dried yellow lentils, soaked in water overnight, drained, and rinsed well
- 4 cups vegetable broth
- 1 small onion, diced
- 1 carrot, diced
- 1 celery stalk, minced
- 2 teaspoons ground turmeric
- 1 teaspoon garlic powder
- ½ teaspoon sea salt
- ½ teaspoon ground ginger
- ½ teaspoon ground cumin
- ½ teaspoon dried thyme leaves
- ¼ teaspoon ground cinnamon
- 2 cups full-fat coconut milk

1. In your slow cooker, combine the lentils, broth, onion, carrot, celery, turmeric, garlic, salt, ginger, cumin, thyme, and cinnamon.
2. Cover the cooker and set to low. Cook for 6 to 8 hours.
3. Stir in the coconut milk and serve.

Chapter 10

Desserts

Slow Cooker Apple Pudding Cake

Prep time: 15 minutes | Cook time: 2 hours | Serves 10

- 2 cups all-purpose flour
- 2/3 cup plus 1/4 cup sugar, divided
- 3 teaspoons baking powder
- 1 teaspoon salt
- 1/2 cup cold butter
- 1 cup 2% milk
- 2 medium tart apples, peeled and chopped
- 1 1/2 cups orange juice
- 1/2 cup honey
- 2 tablespoons butter, melted
- 1 teaspoon ground cinnamon
- 1 1/3 cups sour cream
- 1/4 cup confectioners' sugar

1. In a small bowl, combine the flour, 2/3 cup sugar, baking powder and salt. Cut in butter until mixture resembles coarse crumbs. Stir in milk just until moistened. Spread into the bottom of a greased 4- or 5-qt. slow cooker; sprinkle apples over batter.
2. In a small bowl, combine the orange juice, honey, melted butter, cinnamon and remaining sugar; pour over apples. Cover and cook on high for 2-3 hours or until apples are tender.
3. In a small bowl, combine sour cream and confectioners' sugar. Serve with warm pudding cake.

Fresh Apricot Jam

Prep time: 10 minutes | Cook time: 2 1/2 hours, | Serves 4

- 3 pounds peeled, pitted, and chopped fresh apricots (about 4 1/2 cups)
- 2 tablespoons fresh lemon juice
- One 1.75- or 2-ounce box powdered pectin (optional)
- 3 cups sugar, or to taste

1. Combine the apricots and lemon juice in the slow cooker. Sprinkle with the pectin, if using. Let stand for 20 to 30 minutes.
2. Stir in the sugar. Cover and cook on LOW for 2 1/2 hours, stirring twice during cooking.
3. Remove the lid, turn the cooker to HIGH, and cook for 2 to 4 hours longer, until the jam achieves the desired consistency.
4. Ladle the warm jam into clean spring-top glass jars (or use screw tops with new lids); let stand until cool. Store, covered, in the refrigerator for up to 6 weeks. Or spoon into small plastic storage containers and freeze for up to 3 months.

Rhubarb-Strawberry Compote

Prep time: 10 minutes | Cook time: 3 to 4 hours | Serves 4

- 1/4 cup water or orange juice
- 1 cup sugar
- 1 pound fresh rhubarb, trimmed of leaves and cut into 1 1/2-inch chunks (about 4 cups)
- 2 teaspoons fresh lemon juice
- 2 pints fresh strawberries, hulled and cut in half

1. Combine the water, sugar, and rhubarb in the slow cooker. Cover and cook on LOW until soft, 3 to 4 hours.
2. Mash the rhubarb a bit with a fork or the back of a large spoon. Add the lemon juice and strawberries and stir once to distribute. Turn off the cooker and let the fruit cool a bit.
3. Serve warm or at room temperature. Or transfer to a storage container, refrigerate, and serve chilled, ladled into dessert bowls. The compote will keep, tightly covered, for 4 days in the refrigerator.

Easy Chocolate Cheesecake

Prep time: 30 minutes | Cook time: 10 minutes | Serves 2

For the Cheesecake:
- 2 ½ tbsp. sour cream
- 3 tbsp. erythritol powder
- 5 tbsp. cream cheese
- 3 tbsp. cocoa powder
- 2 tbsp. butter
- ½ tsp. vanilla extract

For the Crust:
- 2 tbsp. almond flour
- a pinch of kosher salt
- 2 tsp. cocoa powder
- 2 tsp. butter
- 2 tsp. powdered Erythritol

1. To make the crust, roast the almond flour in a pan over medium heat until golden, about 3 minutes.
2. Pour the roasted almond flour into a small bowl. Then add in the cocoa, sweetener, and salt.
3. Add the butter and mix well.
4. Press the mixture into a pastry mold or a plate and then refrigerate while the cheesecake is being prepared.
5. To make the cheesecake, put the sour cream in a medium bowl and beat with an electric mixer for 3 minutes.
6. Add the cream cheese and butter and beat with an electric mixer until the cream is completely mixed.
7. Add the vanilla extract, sweetener, and cocoa. Beat until everything is mixed together.
8. Pour the mixture into the mold. Freeze for 20–30 minutes.

Chocolate Chip Brownie

Prep time: 20 minutes | Cook time: 15 minutes | Serves 2

- ½ cup MCT oil
- 2 tsp. Erythritol
- ½ cup water
- ¼ tsp. baking powder
- 1 tsp. vanilla extract
- ¼ tsp. salt
- ½ cup coconut flour
- 1 cup Keto chocolate chips
- 2 tbsp. cocoa powder

1. Mix 1 tbsp. of cocoa powder and 1 tbsp. of MCT oil. Mix well. Add a few drops of vanilla extract and sweetener. Mix them well.
2. Preheat the oven to 356°C. Put the MCT oil, water, vanilla extract, coconut flour, chocolate chips, salt, baking powder, and sweetener into a bowl. Mix them all well. Let it cool for at least 10 minutes before baking.
3. Cover the pan with parchment paper. Stir the mixture in the pan. Bake for 15 minutes. Allow the brownies to cool for 10 minutes before slicing and serving.

Spiced Sweet Potato Pudding

Prep time: 15 minutes | Cook time: 3 hours | Serves 7

- 2 cans (15 3/4 ounces each) sweet potatoes, drained and mashed
- 3 eggs
- 1 can (12 ounces) evaporated milk
- $2/3$ cup biscuit/baking mix
- $1/2$ cup packed brown sugar
- $1/2$ cup apple butter
- 2 tablespoons butter, softened
- 2 teaspoons vanilla extract
- $1/3$ cup finely chopped pecans
- pound cake, optional

1. In a large bowl, beat the first eight until well-blended. Pour into a greased 3-qt. slow cooker. Sprinkle with pecans.
2. Cover and cook on low for 3-4 hours or until a thermometer reads 160°. Serve with pound cake if desired.

Caramel Pear Pudding

Prep time: 20 minutes | Cook time: 3 hours | Serves 10

- 1 cup all-purpose flour
- $1/2$ cup sugar
- 1 $1/2$ teaspoons baking powder
- $1/2$ teaspoon ground cinnamon
- $1/4$ teaspoon salt
- $1/8$ teaspoon ground cloves
- $1/2$ cup 2% milk
- 4 medium pears, peeled and cubed
- $1/2$ cup chopped pecans
- $3/4$ cup packed brown sugar
- $1/4$ cup butter, softened
- $1/2$ cup boiling water
- vanilla ice cream, optional

1. In a large bowl, combine flour, sugar, baking powder, cinnamon, salt and cloves. Stir in milk until smooth. Add pears and pecans. Spread evenly into a 3-qt. slow cooker coated with cooking spray.
2. In a small bowl, combine brown sugar and butter; stir in boiling water. Pour over batter (do not stir). Cover and cook on low for 3-4 hours or until pears are tender. Serve warm with ice cream if desired.

Slow Cooker Baked Apples

Prep time: 25 minutes | Cook time: 4 hours | Serves 6

- 6 medium tart apples
- 1/2 cup raisins
- 1/3 cup packed brown sugar
- 1 tablespoon grated orange peel
- 1 cup water
- 3 tablespoons thawed orange juice concentrate
- 2 tablespoons butter

1. Core apples and peel top third of each if desired. Combine the raisins, brown sugar and orange peel; spoon into apples. Place in a 5-qt. slow cooker.
2. Pour water around apples. Drizzle with orange juice concentrate. Dot with butter. Cover and cook on low for 4-5 hours or until apples are tender.

Fruity Delight Cake

Prep time: 10 minutes | Cook time: 2-3 hours | Serves 8-10

- 20-oz. can crushed pineapple
- 21-oz. can blueberry **or** cherry pie filling
- 18½-oz. pkg. yellow cake mix
- cinnamon
- ½ cup butter
- 1 cup chopped nuts

1. Grease bottom and sides of slow cooker.
2. Spread layers of pineapple, blueberry pie filling, and dry cake mix. Be careful not to mix the layers.
3. Sprinkle with cinnamon.
4. Top with thin layers of butter chunks and nuts.
5. Cover. Cook on High 2-3 hours.
6. Serve with vanilla ice cream.

Stewed Blueberries

Prep time: 10 minutes | Cook time: 3 to 4 hours | Serves 4

- 4 cups fresh or frozen blueberries
- 1/2 cup sugar
- 1/3 cup orange juice
- 3 slices lemon

1. Add all the ingredients to the slow cooker and stir to combine. Cover and let stand at room temperature for 15 minutes or in the refrigerator for an hour to give the berries a chance to exude some liquid (this is especially important for the frozen berries).
2. Cook on LOW for 3 to 4 hours. Turn off the cooker, remove the lid, and let the blueberries cool a bit. Serve warm or at room temperature. Or transfer to a storage container, refrigerate, and serve chilled, ladled into dessert bowls. The blueberries will keep, tightly covered, for 4 days in the refrigerator.

Fresh Bing Cherry Jam

Prep time: 10 minutes | Cook time: 2 1/2 hours | Serves 4

- 4 cups pitted fresh Bing cherries from about 2 pounds of cherries (you will have both whole and pieces of cherries)
- 2 cups sugar
- 2 tablespoons fresh lemon juice
- Pinch of salt
- 3 tablespoons powdered pectin

1. Combine the cherries, sugar, lemon juice, and salt in the slow cooker. Let stand for 15 minutes to dissolve the sugar.
2. Sprinkle with the pectin. Cover and cook on LOW for 2 1/2 hours, stirring twice during cooking.
3. Remove the lid, turn the cooker to HIGH, and cook for 2 to 3 hours longer, until the jam reaches your desired consistency.
4. Ladle the warm jam into clean spring-top glass jars (or use screw tops with new lids); let stand until cool. Store, covered, in the refrigerator for up to 2 months. Or spoon into small plastic storage containers and freeze for up to 3 months.

Choco Lava Cake

Prep time: 15 minutes | Cook time: 10 minutes | Serves 2

- 1 oz. dark chocolate
- 1 tbsp. almond flour
- ¼ cup coconut oil
- ¼ tsp. vanilla extract
- 2 eggs
- Cocoa powder, for garnishing
- 2 tbsp. sweetener

1. Preheat the oven to 374°C. Grease 2 molds with coconut oil and sprinkle them with cocoa powder. Melt the chocolate in the coconut and then add in the vanilla. Beat the eggs and the sweetener together in a different bowl.
2. Slowly, add the chocolate mixture to the egg mixture and beat until well mixed. Then add the almond flour and mix until incorporated. Fill the molds evenly with the mixture. Bake for 10 minutes. Serve immediately.

Stuffed Sweet Onions

Prep time: 45 minutes | Cook time: 4 hours | Serves 4

- 4 medium sweet onions
- 2 small zucchini, shredded
- 1 large garlic clove, minced
- 1 tablespoon olive oil
- 1 teaspoon dried basil
- 1 teaspoon dried thyme
- ¼ teaspoon salt
- ¼ teaspoon pepper
- ½ cup dry bread crumbs
- 4 thick-sliced bacon strips, cooked and crumbled
- ¼ cup grated Parmesan cheese
- ¼ cup reduced-sodium chicken broth

1. Peel onions and cut a ¼-in. slice from the top and bottom. Carefully cut and remove the center of each onion, leaving a ½-in. shell; chop removed onion.
2. In a large skillet, saute the zucchini, garlic and chopped onions in oil until tender and juices are reduced. Stir in the basil, thyme, salt and pepper.
3. Remove from the heat. Stir in the bread crumbs, bacon and Parmesan cheese. Fill onion shells with the zucchini mixture.
4. Place in a greased 3- or 4-qt. slow cooker. Add broth to the slow cooker. Cover and cook on low for 4-5 hours or until onions are tender.

Rum-Butterscotch Bananas

Prep time: 10 minutes | **Cook time:** 1 1/4 to 2 1/2 hours | **Serves 4**

- 1/2 cup (1 stick) unsalted butter
- 1/2 cup firmly packed light brown sugar
- Combine the butter, brown sugar, and rum in the slow cooker. Cover and cook on LOW for 1 to 1 1/4 cup dark rum
- 2 large, firm, ripe bananas
- Vanilla ice cream for serving

1. Combine the butter, brown sugar, and rum in the slow cooker. Cover and cook on LOW for 1 to 1 1/2 hours. Stir with a whisk until smooth.
2. Just before serving, peel the bananas, cut in half lengthwise, and cut each piece in half crosswise to make 4 pieces per banana. Add to the hot sauce. Cover and continue to cook on LOW until heated through and coated with the sauce, 15 to 20 minutes.
3. Serve immediately over scoops of vanilla ice cream.

Slow-Cooked Bread Pudding

Prep time: 15 minutes | **Cook time:** 3 hours | **Serves 8**

- 4 whole wheat bagels, split and cut into 3/4-inch pieces
- 1 large tart apple, peeled and chopped
- 1/2 cup dried cranberries
- 1/4 cup golden raisins
- 2 cups fat-free milk
- 1 cup egg substitute
- 1/2 cup sugar
- 2 tablespoons butter, melted
- 1 teaspoon ground cinnamon
- 1 teaspoon vanilla extract

1. In a 3-qt. slow cooker coated with cooking spray, combine the bagels, apple, cranberries and raisins. In a large bowl, whisk the milk, egg substitute, sugar, butter, cinnamon and vanilla. Pour over bagel mixture and stir to combine; gently press bagels down into milk mixture.
2. Cover and cook on low for 3-4 hours or until a knife inserted near the center comes out clean.

Lemon Poppy Seed Upside-Down Cake

Prep time: 10-15 minutes | **Cook time:** 2-2½ hours | **Serves 8-10**

- 1 pkg. lemon poppy seed bread mix
- 1 egg
- 8 ozs. light sour cream
- ½ cup water

Sauce:
- 1 tbsp. butter
- ¾ cup water
- ½ cup sugar
- ¼ cup lemon juice

1. Combine first four ingredients until well moistened. Spread in lightly greased slow cooker.
2. Combine sauce ingredients in small saucepan. Bring to boil. Pour boiling mixture over batter.
3. Cover. Cook on High 2-2½ hours. Edges will be slightly brown. Turn heat off and leave in cooker for 30 minutes with cover slightly ajar.
4. When cool enough to handle, hold a large plate over top of cooker, then invert.
5. Allow to cool before slicing.

Coconut Cupcakes

Prep time: 15 minutes | Cook time: 20–30 minutes | Serves 2

Cupcakes:
- 6 tbsp. coconut flour
- ½ cup hot water
- ½ cup unsalted coconut butter
- 1 tsp. vanilla extract
- 1 tbsp. flaxseed
- 1 tsp. baking powder
- 4 tbsp. stevia
- A pinch salt
- dried coconut, optional

For the Icing:
- 1 cup raw cashews
- 2 tbsp. Swerve®
- ½ cup whole coconut milk
- 1 tsp. vanilla extract

1. To make the cupcakes, preheat the oven to 338°C. Grease 6 cupcake molds. Pour the water over the coconut butter and mix well. Then add the flaxseed, vanilla, stevia, and salt. Leave the flaxseed for few minutes to stow everything. In another bowl, mix the baking powder and coconut flour.
2. Add the flour mixture and the flaxseed mixture slowly and stir until no lumps are left and everything is smooth. Spread them in molds and bake for 20–25 minutes, or until the top is solid and the edges turn golden. Then take them out of the oven and wait a few minutes for them to cool
3. To make the icing, put all the ingredients in a blender and blend for about 2–3 minutes, or until smooth. Then add the icing to the cupcakes. Sprinkle with the dried coconut if you want.

Fig and Ginger Jam

Prep time: 10 minutes | Cook time: 2 1/2 hours | Serves 4

- 2 pounds fresh figs, stemmed, peeled, and quartered
- 1 1/2 cups sugar
- 1/2 cup water
- 1 thin-skinned lemon, quartered and thinly sliced (remove any seeds)
- 2 tablespoons chopped crystallized ginger

1. Combine the figs, sugar, water, lemon, and ginger in the slow cooker. Cover and cook on LOW for 2 1/2 hours, stirring twice during cooking.
2. Remove the lid, turn the cooker to HIGH, and cook for 2 to 3 hours longer, until the jam reaches your desired consistency.
3. Ladle the warm jam into clean spring-top glass jars (or use screw tops with new lids); let stand until cool. Store, covered, in the refrigerator for up to 2 months. Or spoon into small plastic storage containers and freeze for up to 3 months.

Appendix 1 Measurement Conversion Chart

Volume Equivalents (Dry)

US STANDARD	METRIC (APPROXIMATE)
1/8 teaspoon	0.5 mL
1/4 teaspoon	1 mL
1/2 teaspoon	2 mL
3/4 teaspoon	4 mL
1 teaspoon	5 mL
1 tablespoon	15 mL
1/4 cup	59 mL
1/2 cup	118 mL
3/4 cup	177 mL
1 cup	235 mL
2 cups	475 mL
3 cups	700 mL
4 cups	1 L

Volume Equivalents (Liquid)

US STANDARD	US STANDARD (OUNCES)	METRIC (APPROXIMATE)
2 tablespoons	1 fl.oz.	30 mL
1/4 cup	2 fl.oz.	60 mL
1/2 cup	4 fl.oz.	120 mL
1 cup	8 fl.oz.	240 mL
1 1/2 cup	12 fl.oz.	355 mL
2 cups or 1 pint	16 fl.oz.	475 mL
4 cups or 1 quart	32 fl.oz.	1 L
1 gallon	128 fl.oz.	4 L

Temperatures Equivalents

FAHRENHEIT(F)	CELSIUS(C) APPROXIMATE)
225 °F	107 °C
250 °F	120 ° °C
275 °F	135 °C
300 °F	150 °C
325 °F	160 °C
350 °F	180 °C
375 °F	190 °C
400 °F	205 °C
425 °F	220 °C
450 °F	235 °C
475 °F	245 °C
500 °F	260 °C

Weight Equivalents

US STANDARD	METRIC (APPROXIMATE)
1 ounce	28 g
2 ounces	57 g
5 ounces	142 g
10 ounces	284 g
15 ounces	425 g
16 ounces (1 pound)	455 g
1.5 pounds	680 g
2 pounds	907 g

Appendix 2 The Dirty Dozen and Clean Fifteen

The Environmental Working Group (EWG) is a nonprofit, nonpartisan organization dedicated to protecting human health and the environment Its mission is to empower people to live healthier lives in a healthier environment. This organization publishes an annual list of the twelve kinds of produce, in sequence, that have the highest amount of pesticide residue-the Dirty Dozen-as well as a list of the fifteen kinds of produce that have the least amount of pesticide residue-the Clean Fifteen.

THE DIRTY DOZEN

The 2016 Dirty Dozen includes the following produce. These are considered among the year's most important produce to buy organic:

Strawberries	Spinach
Apples	Tomatoes
Nectarines	Bell peppers
Peaches	Cherry tomatoes
Celery	Cucumbers
Grapes	Kale/collard greens
Cherries	Hot peppers

The Dirty Dozen list contains two additional items kale/collard greens and hot peppers-because they tend to contain trace levels of highly hazardous pesticides.

THE CLEAN FIFTEEN

The least critical to buy organically are the Clean Fifteen list. The following are on the 2016 list:

Avocados	Papayas
Corn	Kiw
Pineapples	Eggplant
Cabbage	Honeydew
Sweet peas	Grapefruit
Onions	Cantaloupe
Asparagus	Cauliflower
Mangos	

Some of the sweet corn sold in the United States are made from genetically engineered (GE) seedstock. Buy organic varieties of these crops to avoid GE produce.

Appendix 3 Index

A
allspice 26
almond milk 10, 23, 29, 67, 83
almonds 16, 17, 26, 27, 31, 46, 77
apple 10, 15, 18, 71, 77, 79

B
bacon 19, 23, 25, 37, 38, 55, 56, 59
baking soda 18, 87
balsamic vinegar 62, 69
basil 17, 24, 25, 28, 33, 34, 37
bell pepper 23, 28, 32, 42, 71, 72, 78
bread 19, 22, 24, 28, 38, 81, 82, 83, 84, 85
broccoli 21, 23, 25, 28, 73

C
canola oil 87
carrot 32, 67
cauliflower 10, 17, 19, 56, 64, 67, 71
cayenne pepper 21, 29, 31, 45, 54
cheese 9, 10, 12, 13, 14, 15, 16, 18, 21
chives 14, 19, 25, 52, 76, 78
cinnamon 10, 13, 15, 17, 18, 26, 27
coconut cream 29, 31, 38, 42
coriander 32, 39, 56, 78, 79
cranberries 10, 86
custard 81, 82, 83, 85

D
dark rum 15, 83
Dijon mustard 39, 62
dried cherries 48, 85

E
egg 14, 22, 23, 25, 27, 28, 32, 44, 81, 82
erythritol 26, 81, 86, 87

F
flour 10, 13, 17, 18, 29, 32, 37, 41, 52
fresh chives 14, 19, 25, 76, 78
fresh parsley 16, 29, 31, 46, 47, 48

G
garlic 11, 13, 15, 16, 18, 21, 22, 23, 24, 25, 26, 28, 31
Greek yogurt 59, 81

H
halves 32, 34, 36, 37
hazelnuts 59
honey 14, 27, 45, 79

J
juice 15, 19, 31, 33, 35, 37, 38, 39, 42, 43, 50

K
kale 67, 69, 72, 77
ketchup 43

L
lemon 15, 19, 31, 34, 35, 38, 54, 73, 78, 81, 83, 86
lemon juice 15, 35, 38, 54, 73, 78, 81

90 | *The XXL Slow Cooker Cookbook*

lime 37, 39, 42, 43, 50, 51, 56, 57
lime juice 37, 39, 43, 50, 51, 58, 79, 87
lime zest 42, 57

M

mango 79
maple syrup 10, 13, 27, 62
mesh sieve 15, 41, 51
milk 10, 13, 14, 19, 22, 23, 24, 25, 26, 28, 29
minced fresh chives 14, 19, 25, 78
Mozzarella cheese 56, 59
muffins 83

N

Nutella 85
nuts 62, 87

O

olive oil 9, 12, 14, 15, 16, 21, 25, 26, 31, 32, 35, 37
onion 11, 13, 16, 21, 22, 23, 24, 25, 26, 28, 31, 32, 33, 34, 35, 38, 39, 41, 42, 45, 49, 50
orange juice 31, 79
oregano 10, 16, 22, 31, 32, 33, 35, 37, 39, 42

P

paprika 10, 12, 23, 25, 27, 37, 38, 42
Parmesan cheese 18, 23, 29, 70, 74, 76
parsley 16, 23, 29, 31, 34, 38, 44, 46, 47, 48
pepper flakes 11, 16, 33, 47, 49, 50, 60, 76

pudding 81, 82, 83, 85
pumpkin 26, 82

R

raisins 15, 27, 33, 43, 46, 83, 84
red pepper flakes 11, 16, 33, 47, 49, 50, 60, 76
rice 8, 11, 12, 34, 35, 36, 37, 46, 56, 62, 63, 64, 66, 71, 78, 83, 84
ricotta cheese 25, 26, 87

S

salt 11, 12, 13, 14, 15, 16, 18, 19, 22, 23, 24, 25, 26, 27, 28, 31, 32, 33, 34, 35, 36, 37, 38
shrimp 54, 56, 57, 58, 59, 60
sugar 10, 11, 12, 13, 15, 16, 17, 18, 19, 21, 27, 41, 42, 43, 45, 47, 48, 62, 69, 71, 79, 81, 82, 83, 84, 85, 87

T

tomato 16, 25, 31, 33, 35, 39, 43, 47, 49, 50, 58, 59, 60, 62, 73, 76

V

vanilla yogurt 87
vegetable broth 23, 48, 56, 62, 63

W

white wine 8, 9, 12, 14, 31, 35, 36, 55

Y

yogurt 59, 78, 81, 87

The XXL Slow Cooker Cookbook | 91

Sarah J. Joyner

Printed in Great Britain
by Amazon